Behavior Analysis and Interviewing Techniques B.A.I.T

Steven Varnell

ISBN 0985382112

ISBN 978-0-9853821-1-7

Also by Steven Varnell
Criminal Interdiction
Tactical Survival

To those brave souls that have suffered the ultimate sacrifice for the rest of us, whether we were deserving of such sacrifice or not. Still you stepped into the streets and gave it all.

CONTENTS

Surprise? It's only in the mind of the victim. Surprise is simply the perception that something (an event and/or the process by which it changes) is happening contrary to expectations.

-------------Barton S Whaley

INTRODUCTION

Since the release of *Criminal Interdiction* and *Tactical Survival,* I have wanted to write a book about human behaviors and interviewing. My goal has been to discover how I could write a book on interviewing and still give the topic an original foundation. After all, few topics are covered more than these. Another requirement is the new book has to be in an area of officer survival and safety.

I have initiated a series of lecture based training courses derived from the books and they are currently presented nationwide. Together with former partners, I have started our new instructional group called Interdiction and Survival Strategies (ISS). Instructing your peers is hard enough, teaching new concepts to law enforcement officers is another category by itself. A vast amount of time has been invested into the research for this book to make it a topic that anyone will look forward to receiving.

Behavior Analysis and Interviewing Techniques (BAIT) takes us deep into the minds of suspects while seeking solutions to many of the problems experienced by police officers for effective evaluation and interviewing. I sought out research from around the globe and applied it to my own experiences.

In my 29 plus years in law enforcement, I have completed many Interviews and Interrogation classes, including specialized courses for instructors, and conducted thousands of interviews. Any concepts that deal with the human psyche have always been a favored topic of mine and the foundation of my training courses. The knowledge to be learned can save your life. Safety and survival is the preeminent end result of our job and my writings.

I will introduce you to an actual event which led to the officer's death. Never will or shall any of these accounts be considered a criticism of any officer. Never should anyone read this book and say, "I would never do that!" You need to say to yourself, "I have to do my best to never repeat that situation."

Criminal Interdiction literally was written "off the top of my head." The ideas and chapters were based upon my own experiences. Except for statistical data, little research was required. *Criminal Interdiction* was what I did each day of my career for over 29 years. Officially, I retired from law enforcement on June 30th, 2011, but I never retired mentally; does anyone? The information I retained to recognize and arrest the bad guys continues to this day. Imbedded this deep, no switch can turn off the mental processes. I am not on patrol, but I will always be on the streets. My eyes will always be watching and my mind will always be trying to discover new ways to safely complete various police task. The difference is that now I have the time to conduct research. I read books, research papers, conducted countless interviews, and searched the World Wide Web to make the information "cutting edge."

In *Tactical Survival* we discussed areas of self-defense in ways that are no longer considered yet have a proven track record in combat. As I travel around the country teaching, I learn new ideas. I am asked questions and at times challenged in some of my concepts because some of what I address may be considered controversial. I welcome all ideas, considerations, consultations and complaints. To me this is how the best approach to a situation is obtained. It indicates that they listened and are applying the ideas into their own. Some are convinced and others not sure, yet not one has ever said these ideas will not work and here is why. Many officers have contacted me after reading the books or attending a class. They explain to me about a particular event that occurred and how they overcame the situation by applying what I teach. Now that is excitement of the ultimate degree in my soul.

For me, the learning still continues. Incessantly, I conduct research and make minor adjustments to my presentations. I demand of myself that when lecturing to law enforcement, the information is current and cutting edge because they deserve nothing less. As more information is discovered, I will create expanded chapters in the current books and expound on the information to the courses.

Agree or disagree, pick at the small insignificant issues, complain about layout or a lack of photos, editing errors and what not. This is a book of ideas and learned practices to help you survive and become a better truth seeker. No photo will increase your knowledge like expressive words. As is said so often, a picture is worth a thousand words, but here we let the words become our mental pictures. Stay focused on what is important; the events in front of you during your shift. In the end, be open- minded and at least try the ideas I expose to you. As you read, think how often the small things could have changed the outcome of so many events.

Behavior Analysis and Interviewing Techniques, (BAIT) is a new approach to the topic and I hope it finds its way into the minds of officers everywhere. Use the BAIT acronym to help you remember that first we observe their behaviors and then we recognize their deceptions through effective interviewing. BAIT is a process of effective criminal recognition and investigation. I know the techniques work and I am certain the foundations are sound because I tested them for decades. Experiment with them with an open mind. See how they stand up to your own ideas. If you are not pleased with one, change it to meet your needs. The end result is still a success. What I ask is to be flexible and understand that not one of us has all of the answers, but we can always improve. Incorporate them into your own techniques and have fun taking out the bad guys.

In 2011, the United States Department of Justice, COPS Program, released their "Officer Safety and Wellness" Report by Mora L. Fielder. It describes many things about our changing society and the propensity of criminals to use a firearm leading to a potentially more dangerous work environment for law enforcement. There was an area of the report that caught my eye and I agree with wholeheartedly. This is the quote from the report in regards to training:

"Training is another fundamental factor for officer safety, health, and wellness and thus is not the area to cut corners or cost. It should be the primary investment made by an organization. Yet, when economic times tighten budgets, training is usually the first to be eliminated. Most agencies have annual hours dedicated for in-service training, but often the additional or advanced training opportunities are what enhance officer knowledge, minimize risks or mistakes, and help hone duty-specific skills, knowledge, and abilities. Tactical training enables officers to keep honing skills such as driving, handling violent encounters, and operating less than lethal or lethal weapons."

"Violent encounters are one of the most hazardous risks for officers. Attacks can be direct, physical, or with weapons. Constant training and practicing techniques that prepare officers for situations such as these are crucial in safeguarding their lives."

We can never train or study to learn new ideas enough. If your agency will not provide everything, it's up to you alone to seek out the best techniques to help complete the job. Many will complain that if the Department will not provide it, I must not need it. I hope those words do not come back to haunt and follow you to the hospital after you responded ineffectively or worse when you or your fellow officer's ass is on the line.

There are many books on the market today that explains various ideas of interviewing and interrogations. Many more cover body language when it applies to everyday personal situations. Good books are available by former law enforcement officials which discuss body language in terms that a civilian can understand. For the street officer, uniformed or not, there is a need for understanding verbal and nonverbal communications as it relates to safety. No other person has to conduct more interviews and be as observant to behaviors as a police officer. Throughout the course of their day, they will encounter people through traffic stops, pedestrian encounters, accident scenes, crime scenes, domestic calls, and more. Never has another job needed more guidance than that of the police officer. For many members, they have the advantage of moving the interviews into special interrogation rooms. Barren of anything other than chairs and a desk, with a surreptitious audio video system, designed to create an uncomfortable environment for the person interviewed. Once completed, they have time to review the tapes and have other officers watching the interviews from another room. Information can be collected and ideas brought about by all of the people involved. This is an important aspect of acquiring a good confession. These same investigators will go to the field and interview people at other locations, involving various cases, but time is on their side.

For a street cop, time is often against them. It does not take long before dispatch calls them on the radio wanting to know how long before they complete their assignment because other calls are holding. Rapid recognition of certain behaviors is a must. As we have seen, a second can mean the difference between life and death or injury for a street officer. Within this time frame we can develop recognition and motor skills to recognize in advance an action for which a proper response will succeed.

For these very reasons I wrote *Criminal Interdiction*. Because of these exact threats I wrote *Tactical Survival*. For this very cause I am presenting *Behavior Analysis and Interviewing Techniques or BAIT.*

Share your thoughts and experiences with me at criminalinterdiction@live.com. Information about the classes can be found at isstraining.yolasite.com. "Remember, the job entails more than most realize and produces a brotherhood that few understand."

Pelham, Alabama

*What we have done for ourselves alone dies with us;
what we have done for others and the world remains and
is immortal.*

> Albert Pike, a 19th century attorney,
> Confederate Officer and writer

December 2009 in Pelham, Alabama, people were just getting over the Thanksgiving holidays and preparing for Christmas. The weather is getting colder and everyone can feel the excitement of another year ending. Houses around town are decorated with lights and manger scenes. Plastic reindeers and Santa Claus' stood on rooftops and in yards. The feeling around town is growing festive. Smoke rises from the chimney tops as the smell of burning wood lingered in the air. The combination of the sights and smells adds to the excitement as everyone's favorite holiday approached.

Pelham is an upscale city south of Birmingham just off of Interstate 65. It is a quiet place where little happens when compared to the big city crime 20 miles to the north. Housing cost and income is above the states average and below the poverty levels. Pelham is a good place to live and raise a family. The Pelham Police Department employs less than 100 people and is considered a progressive agency. Statistics show that from 2000-2008; there were only four (4) murders within the city limits. The largest percentages of crimes involve thefts and burglaries.

Pelham Police Officer Philip Davis has been on the force for four and half years. Before joining the Pelham Police Department, he worked with the Calera Police Department and the University of Alabama Police Department. Officer Davis is part of the Departments training program. Not only is he involved with his own agency, like most officers, he also takes a personal interest in the betterment of the community. Davis teaches women's self-defense classes at Valley Christian Church in Birmingham. He is a Christian man and a proud officer. Again, the city of Pelham has attracted a good officer.

2009 had been a difficult year on law enforcement. On March 24th, four Oakland, California Police Officers are killed by a lone gunman. The next month, on April 4[th,] three Pittsburgh, Pennsylvania Police Officers are killed in a gunfight. Then just days earlier, the 29th of November, four Lakewood Police Officers in Washington State, are gunned down by a psychotic paroled killer. The death of our countries law enforcement officers is again above the yearly average.

On Thursday, December 3, Davis began his shift earlier in the afternoon. He later drove to Interstate 65, a north/south interstate highway which starts in Mobile, Alabama and ends in Gary, Indiana. At about 11:50pm, he's monitoring traffic on the highway when he clocks a gold colored Acura speeding in a construction zone. Davis proceeded to make a traffic stop. Still fresh in his mind is the deadly events of Lakewood, Washington. That day affected Davis as it had all of us in law enforcement with a touch of shock. Davis writes in Facebook his feelings about the incident. Thoughts of each of these incidents were in my mind. I wondered how so many of us could continue to be killed in these senseless acts of rage.

Davis catches up to the speeding Acura which he had clocked at 76 miles per hour (mph) in a posted 55 mph zone. A traffic stop is conducted between the 242 and 243 mile marker. The 242 mile marker is the exit from Interstate 65 to the city of Pelham. It is also known as Shelby County exit 52, the former exit number. The exit numbers for interstate systems have been changed to the mile marker where they make locating easier in times of an emergency. The driver of the Acura pulls off to the right side of the road onto the emergency shoulder and stops. Davis exits his patrol car and approaches the driver's window of the car. He sees that the driver is the only occupant. Davis is wearing a microphone and has a dash mounted video camera in his car. The events that follow are strange, unprovoked, unnecessary, and conducted by the one person no one would have ever suspected.

Unexplained Evil

2

      Bart Wayne Johnson is driving on Interstate 65. He is a pharmacist in the town of Jasper, located 40 miles northwest of Birmingham. Johnson lives in Kimberly, 38 miles north of Pelham or 34 miles east of Jasper, and is married with two children. His wife Dana is also a pharmacist. His salary alone is over $100,000.00 per year. They live in an upscale neighborhood and their house is decorated with lights and plastic candy canes in anticipation of Christmas. He is a graduate of Samford University, School of Pharmacy in Birmingham. Johnson has a brother in law enforcement. He is a police officer in the city of Trussville, a small town 15 miles northeast of Birmingham off of Interstate 59 in Alabama. You can definitely say that Johnson has spreading roots in the area.

      Bart Johnson is considered by his employers as a "go to guy." You can count on him "in a pinch." He understood the day to day operations of a pharmacy. Fred's Pharmacy is scheduled to open a new store in Bayou LaBatre located off Interstate 10, down near the coast of Alabama with the Gulf of Mexico. Because of his understanding of the required work and policies of the company, Bart is asked to travel and help prepare the store for their grand opening. He agrees and is scheduled to be there for several days. He arrives on November 30th and intends to stay until December 3rd to travel back home. While working there he is considered "energetic" and as said by another co-worker, "He kept me going." There were no signs of trouble, anxiety, headaches or other ailments. He worked the same hours as everyone else in their efforts to make the pharmacy grand opening successful.

On his last scheduled day, Bart Johnson had already checked out of his hotel and gone to work. The day is December 3, 2009 and he is ready to go home. It is another long day of work which ends between 8:00 and 8:30pm. He walks to the parking lot with another pharmacist from the new store and they say their goodbyes. Johnson has a few more hours of driving to reach his home north of Birmingham. Before getting in his car, Johnson tells the co-worker, "I don't know if I will make it all the way home tonight." It is not a premonition, but a statement that anyone would make when they are tired and still have a long drive ahead. In this case though, it is the truth and not one that anyone expected.

Bart Johnson travels north from Fred's Pharmacy located on N. Wintzell Ave. onto Highway 188 and then west on Interstate 10. He picks up Interstate 65 northbound for the trip home. This is the start of Interstate 65 and is designated as mile marker 0. Pelham is at mile marker 242 or 242 miles north. The speed limit is 65mph but increases to 70 around Saraland. It slows again around Montgomery and varies the remainder of the trip. Near Pelham, there is road construction and the speed limit has been reduced to 55 mph. He should arrive in the Pelham area around midnight.

A *Routine* Traffic Stop

Pelham Police Officer Philip Davis drives to Interstate 65 to work traffic enforcement. He sets up to run radar and clocks a northbound Acura at 76mph, 21 mph above the speed limit. He accelerates and conducts a traffic stop of this speeding car between the 242 and 243 mm. The car has an Alabama tag number of "JCREW1." The driver of the car activates the turn signal and moves to the outside shoulder of the road. He never takes his foot off the brake. He turns on his vehicles interior lights as Officer Davis approaches on the drivers' side of the car. The Officer explains to the driver that he has stopped him for speeding. He proceeds to ask him if he has his drivers' license and if the car belongs to him. Sarcastically, the driver replies "no, I just stole it." Officer Davis responds in an equal manner and says, "I'm glad you are in a jovial mood." He proceeds to tell the driver that he asked the question because sometimes when people borrow someone's car, they do not know where the proof of insurance is. He then tells the driver, "I'll be right back."

Officer Davis returns to his police car. He writes out the majority of a traffic ticket for unlawful speed. The driver of the car turns out the vehicle interior lights. In his right hand he is holding a Glock .40 caliber handgun. It is tucked under the outside edge of his right leg. Officer Davis returns to the drivers' window of the Acura and asked, "Where do you work?" The driver responds "Why does that matter?" and then tells Officer Davis that his brother is a cop. Davis responds "now he wants to start acting reasonable." He then instructs the driver to have his brother call him and he would explain how he had acted towards him, and "we'll see how that works out."

Pelham Police Officer Philip Davis will not speak again. The driver of the car pulls the .40cal Glock from under his right thigh and shoots Officer Davis in the left side of his face. In fact the bullet enters between his lip and nose, fractured face bones, teeth and fragmented upon striking Officer Davis' spinal cord. He fell straight back with no attempt to catch himself which caused lacerations to the back of his head. The time is 11:57 pm.

A passerby sees Officer Davis go down to the pavement and calls 911. Responding officers to the scene discover the ticket book lying in between Davis' legs. The name of the driver of the car that shot him is Bart Wayne Johnson. On the traffic citation his employment is listed as "Unemployed."

The first person on the scene is a truck driver who sees Officer Davis lying in the outside lane. He stops and runs to the officer. He calls 911 and is told to check for a pulse. He says there is a pulse but no movement. There is a gurgling sound coming from Officer Davis' mouth "almost like he was trying to speak." Other Officers begin to arrive at the scene and start CPR. Another Officer states that there's no pulse, his eyes are open and fixed, and blood from his head runs across both northbound lanes of the interstate. In all likelihood, Officer Davis died instantly.

Officer Davis is transported to University of Alabama, Birmingham hospital where he is pronounced dead. The clock has passed midnight and the date is now 4 December 2009. Davis becomes the first Pelham Police officer killed in the line of duty in the city's 45 year history.

Another officer, family man, dedicated civil servant has passed at the hands of evil. His death takes a small part from each of us with him. The job entails more than most realize and produces a brotherhood that few understand.

Reviewing the video tape from the dash mounted camera of Officer Davis' car, investigators are able to see the events unfold. The brake lights went out 2 seconds after the gunshot and the Acura drove away northbound 6 seconds from the shooting. At the time of the first traffic stop, Bart Johnson was on the phone with his brother, the City of Trussville Police Officer. A few moments after murdering Officer Davis, Johnson's brother calls him back and asked if he had gotten a ticket. Bart Johnson responds, "Nope, not this time."

His plan is to travel north and ditch the car before traveling south again. If he can get south of the scene of the crime, most law enforcement efforts will be directed towards the direction he was last seen driving. Additionally, all of the drivers and vehicle owner's information are for locations north of the crime scene. It makes sense to direct assets to the north of the murder. He had to get rid of the car, the gun, and his shirt because they had Officer Davis' blood on them.

After midnight in the early morning hours of December 4th, a woman is making coffee in her home. She lives in the area of Birmingham known as Inglenook, located on the north side of Birmingham near the airport. It is a low income and low cost housing area. The average home sells below $50,000.00; 4 times below the average home cost of Birmingham. She hears a squealing noise outside and walks to the window. She watches as "a white man" stepped out of a car and starts to walk down the sidewalk towards her home. It's too dark to recognize the man, but he steps into her yard and tries to open her daughters' car door. The door is locked. She opens her front door and questions the man trying to break into the car. He looks up and motions her to go back inside; frightened, she did. At once, she calls the police and tells them about this man who is trying to get into her daughters car. He does not care that he is being watched. She tells the 911 operator that the tag on the car driven by the stranger is "JCREW1." The police tell

8

her that the man outside is a suspect in another incident and instruct her to stay inside behind locked doors.

After locking the door she looks outside again. She sees the man walk out into the street towards another vehicle that has arrived. She sees the man get into the passenger's side of the vehicle described as a gray colored Toyota Tundra pickup truck and together they speed away. She does give the 911 operator a scene by scene description as the events unfold in front of her house, including the full description of the truck. The Acura that the unidentified "white man" had arrived in and the same car stopped by Officer Davis, is left on the side of the street.

A "BOLO" or Be On the Look Out is broadcast to every agency. Cars and motorcycles today are fast, but they can never outrun the radio information broadcast. All known information regarding the car and subsequent events are dispatched across the State of Alabama and the neighboring states.

There is a sick feeling that comes over you when you hear an "officer down" call go out over the radio. At this one moment, all animosities, problems, departmental bickering, dislikes, and inner agency rivalries, dissipate. Officers, Troopers, Deputies, Agents, Detectives, and anyone else, who carries a uniform or a badge, come together. We all know that any homicide is terrible, but the murder of a police officer places it into a different category. Law enforcement officers represent justice, authority, and that barrier between right and wrong. When someone is willing to cause harm to the badge, that person is willing to do anything to anyone. They are at that moment a rabid dog. Every sense of right or wrong has vanished. They have committed an atrocity to the very fiber of our society. Remember that we place ourselves at a much greater risk and are therefore provided greater protections.

There are people who have always taken issue with this topic. It is said that by placing greater penalties against someone who harms a police officer gives the appearance that their life is more valuable. It is a shallow argument that some people will never understand. Remember in *Criminal Interdiction* the story of the sheep and the sheep dog? The sheep always hate the sheep dogs until the wolf shows up. Just as you have seen in every disaster, the public runs from the catastrophe as the police run into them. As I like to say, the job entails more than most realize and produces a brotherhood that few understand.

In the City of Trussville, Alabama, the BOLO information is broadcast. A Trussville officer then ran the "JCREW1" tag and sees the name and address of the registered owner. He knows the car belongs to Bart Johnson, the brother of fellow Trussville Police Department Officer Johnson. The time is now 12:40 am. A Trussville Police supervisor contacts and instructs Officer Johnson on three separate occasions to go to his brother's house in Kimberly. Officer Johnson never goes there. At 1:06 am, the Trussville Police Supervisor is told that Officer Johnson's traveling south on Interstate 65. At 1:30 am, the Trussville Supervisor states that the Acura from the murder scene of Officer Davis has been located near a home in the Inglenook area of Birmingham. Further information is received that the man driving that car has now entered a gray Toyota Tundra pickup truck. The supervisor knows that the Toyota description matches the vehicle driven by Trussville Police Officer Johnson. I can only imagine the confusion and shock befalling everyone involved.

The supervisor then calls his officers and advises that there is now a BOLO for the gray Toyota truck belonging to their officer. A few moments later, a gray Toyota Tundra pickup truck approaches and stops at a roadblock on Highway 31 and Interstate 65 manned by members of the Hoover Police Department. The truck is occupied by the two Johnson brothers. At gunpoint, both men are placed face down onto the ground. The passenger in the truck, Bart Johnson states out loud for the arresting officers to hear, "I'm the one you're looking for." Both men are transported to the Hoover jail in separate cars. In the glove box of the Toyota is found a bloody Glock .40 Cal pistol. Bart Johnsons Acura is located within the City of Birmingham at the location where he tried to steal a car and was picked up by his brother. There is blood on the driver's side door and roof. Later analysis will show it is the blood of Officer Davis.

Bart Johnson is placed into jail on no bond. His neighbors are shocked to hear the news. One states, "They had a nice house, nice cars, a boat, a motorcycle. The only thing missing was the white picket fence. I thought they had it all." We may never know why this happened. "As best I can determine, he didn't like police," says a prosecutor on the case; His brother is an officer. Officer Johnson is released and not charged with any crimes. Though trapped between the natural desires to help a brother, he follows his oath of office. In doing so he stops the madness of the night and saves the life of his brother. He had taken him and turned him over to the authorities.

The actions that were taken by Johnson clearly show that he knew what he was doing and that it was wrong. All of the evasive actions from calling for help, dumping the car, and trying to steal another dashes the idea of temporary insanity. Of course when the case first breaks, there are all types of things running through our mind. Was Bart Johnson transporting illegal drugs? Was he bringing home prescription drugs stolen from the pharmacy? Was he stealing other things from the pharmacy? When stopped by Officer Davis, did he panic with the thoughts of something he had in the car or had recently done? Maybe he was high on illegal drugs or prescription drugs. His defense later would argue that he suffered with migraines and had mixed a migraine medication with alcohol.

It will later be shown in trial that an inventory of the Fred Pharmacy stores showed that nothing was missing. His co-workers, who worked with him during the crucial and difficult week of the store grand opening, testified that Bart Johnson showed no signs of suffering from anything. They never saw him take medications and he never complained of headaches. There were no signs of anything illegal in the car. The arresting officers at the roadblock stated that Johnson did not show any signs of impairment nor complained of any. He was coherent and complied with all instructions.

To commit murder, face to face, and on top of that to commit the murder of a uniformed authority figure is evil. Remember, Bart Johnson was talking to his brother, a police officer, at the time he was stopped.

Why did this happen? There are many reasons and none of them make sense. The facts from his trial are: Bart Wayne Johnson had already received 18 traffic tickets. Even though his own brother is a police officer, he generally dislikes cops. The traffic citation found between the legs of the lifeless body of Officer Davis was his 19th and would have suspended his license. The emotions of the moment had overcome the tired Pharmacist to the point he committed murder over a traffic ticket!

Johnson then had to develop a plan of escape. Why? He knew what he had just committed was wrong and he had to devise a reason that cleared him of the capital punishment act. In my opinion, these are not the actions of someone who suffers from mental illness.

A psychiatrist testifying for the defense asked Johnson about the evening when he was pulled over by Officer Davis. Johnson said that he does not remember much about that night but does say, "I guess I shot him." When asked why, he says he has no idea. Johnson said that he stopped at a McDonalds Restaurant for a coke and mixed it with rum and was taking Imitrex for migraines. When driving, he saw blue lights ahead on the interstate and thought the police were conducting a sting operation to get him. He stated that it felt like he was driving into a cemetery and that is when he called his brother.

When there is not another rational reason and there are no reasons for the act of murder, blame it on illness. He thought he was driving into a sting operation, yet he was speeding. Not trying to outrun anyone or drive overly cautious, just speeding. He pulled over and stopped when he was directed to by the blue lights from Officer Davis' patrol car. He is rude and belligerent towards the officer who is just doing his job. Johnson tries to take another approach by saying his brother is an officer as an attempt to try and get out of the ticket. It is too late. Officer Davis is going to do his job. Nothing else has worked, but Johnson is not taking this ticket. Many things are passing through his mind but only he knows for sure. After killing Officer Davis, Johnson drive's into town to ditch his car. He could later say it was stolen. He could say to investigators, I was not driving the car, it was stolen. I am a Pharmacist, my brother is a cop and I have never done anything wrong except traffic violations. That was until this night when he committed murder.

On May 13, 2011, a jury decided Bart Wayne Johnson was guilty of murder and deserved to die at the hands of the State. Amen.

The cause of this tragedy is the choice made by Bart Johnson. Each event in our lives is determined by the choices we make in response to an event. There are no other reasons that this entire incident occurred except for the delusional acts of Bart Johnson. That said, in no way are the following sentences derogatory to anything that Officer Davis did that night. This never should have happened, but it did. In *Criminal Interdiction* and *Tactical Survival*, I speak at length about the tactics of a traffic stop. There were measures that Officer Davis could have taken to reduce the odds against him. Another event unfolded that we will discuss later that neither Davis nor Johnson realized at the time. Non-intentional, top down Attention Manipulation was directed towards Davis. When Johnson spoke about his law enforcement brother, Davis directed his eyes and attention away. He reached for and looked at a note pad to get the brothers information. This split second occurrence opened the door for Johnson to choose his course of action.

Two families destroyed. Officer Davis leaves behind a wife and two children. The Johnson family is also fatherless now. He leaves a wife and two children behind as well. How does anyone ever explain the actions of December 3, 2009 to any of these children?

In the proud tradition of law enforcement, the memory of Officer Davis is remembered by his family and friends by sharing their love of community. Please visit The Philip Mahan Davis Foundation at http://officerphilipdavis.com/. It is "a not-for-profit organization dedicated to honoring the lives of our fallen heroes. The Foundation provides support and assistance to the families of Alabama Police Officers who were killed or catastrophically injured in the line of duty.

Established in 2011, the Foundation strengthens the relationship between the Alabama Police, its business and civic leaders, and its citizenry. It allows us to express our gratitude to the fallen Officers' families for the ultimate sacrifice of their loved one."

Pelham Police Officer Philip M. Davis

OODA Loop

4

Radical uncertainty is a necessary precondition of physical and mental vitality: all new opportunities and ideas spring from some mismatch between reality and ideas about it.

– Col. John Boyd

Officer safety is paramount in every decision we make. After 29 plus years of working the street, I learned early that understanding the behavioral habits of people can give me the edge needed to overcome the advantages held by the criminals. They know what they are intending to do and have the benefit of surprise, yet still it is up to you to overcome. It is action vs. reaction in which reaction rarely is victorious. To comprehend our ability to overcome this deficit, we need to understand the groundbreaking research and development of the OODA Loop concept. OODA stands for Observe Orient Decide and Act. It is a process which was first developed by USAF Colonel John Boyd. He had developed the Energy-Maneuverability theory (a model of aircraft performance which led to the development of the F15 and 16) based on his observations as a fighter pilot in the Korean War.

Colonel Boyd had an amazing mind in terms of combat strategy. Young pilots always wanted new strategy which led to his first research project called "Fast Transients." It dealt with ones abilities to adjust faster than your opponent to keep them off guard. Later he will re-name it "Patterns of Change" before settling upon the "OODA Loop." Boyd began researching ground combat and was amazed at how so many battles throughout history has been fought when small armies easily defeated vastly superior ones. An example is how the Roman legions lost 70,000 soldiers compared to 3,000 soldiers lost from the armies led by Hannibal and the Carthaginians. He discovered the common thread was that none of the leaders threw their armies head to head against an opponent. They avoided attrition and adapted to maneuverability. Success rested upon their ability to transition quickly from one maneuver to another. He explored the German blitzkrieg and the Israelis attack on Entebbe in Uganda as other shining examples.

I will begin with the concepts behind the OODA loop theory as it can have an effect on every other process we encounter. According to Col. Boyd, decision-making occurs in a recurring cycle of observe-orient-decide-act. Observe – seeing what is happening, Orient – interpreting what is happening, Decide – how to respond to the action, Act – your response to the action taken. The officer who can process this cycle quickly, observing and reacting to the unfolding events faster than an opponent, can thereby "get inside" the opponent's decision cycle and gain the advantage. Boyd developed the concept to explain how to direct one's energies to defeat an adversary and survive. Boyd emphasized that "the loop" is actually a set of interacting loops that are to be kept in continuous operation during combat. He also indicated that the phase of the battle has an important bearing on the ideal allocation of one's energies. In other words, at what point do you understand what is occurring and how fast do you react. An example of this is once a subject starts to draw their weapon on you; they are already at step four of the OODA loop. They have already Observed, Oriented, made the Decision and initiated the Act. You are only on step one or the Observation phase, decidedly behind them. Action beats reaction almost every time. You will never want to play catch up in a gun battle. Your actions have to create pause or confusion which stops their progression to react to yours and will cause them to over or under react to your action. The key to survival is in our ability to adapt to change, not perfect adaptation to existing circumstances. (Doing the same thing over and over and expecting different results). You have to constantly think about if they do this I will do that, an ever evolving and fluid movement. You have to do something fast and unpredictable to keep them off guard

It is also imperative to understand that the Orientation phase is the single most important loop. Orientation is shown to be affected by up to five influences: Cultural traditions, genetic heritage, previous experiences, ability to analyze and react, and processing new information. Because of these factors it is the most important part of the loop since it has an effect on the outcome and shapes the way we observe, decide and act. This is when our training and experience plays the primary role. Everything we do is affected by training and experience. It is through training that we learn what the most effective tactics are and it is discovered through experience what will work. Only when we can observe the threat and based upon our training and experience, orient to the threat and decide the most efficient course of action and act will we be successful. This necessitates the need for not only training, but effective training. We all receive training to meet our standards requirements, but much of the training we receive is not based on reality.

An example of this unrealistic training would be in defensive tactics. Once a year we meet for an 8 hour training session. We are introduced to various holds and grabs similar to MMA style fighting. We are taught defensive measures if we are mounted while on our back. The reality of this, as I have shown with an entire chapter dedicated to this topic in *Tactical Survival*, is that this training will actually place you in jeopardy, not benefit your survival. The tactics taught have to be swift and easy and never should any of us go to the ground with an assailant. The skill necessary to properly learn these tactics requires too much time. As Boyd said, the key to victory is maneuverability not attrition. Never stand toe to toe and battle it out with an assailant. The victory can easily go either way.

True success occurs when we develop the proper feel or reactions for the situations. We want to increase the tempo to bypass the orientation and decision phases. This causes observation and action to occur almost simultaneously. We are in essence compressing time while forcing them to extend time all the while placing them further behind us.

An example of this is when we are driving and the driver in front of us brake's their vehicle. We see and instantly respond by braking ourselves in order to prevent an accident. We observed the action, but we are not required to pass through the orientation and decision phases of the Loop. The action taken is a "known response" to a "known action." It is a process which takes time and practice. Another example is when firing your service weapon and a shell jams. We instantly respond with the "tap, rack, and shoot" method of clearing the weapon.

To help us reach this time compression state, Hick's Law explains the time it takes a person to make a decision as a result of the choices available. It only makes sense that the more choices made available to us the longer it takes to decide which to apply. The more the choices are minimalized, lag time is reduced. This is the imperative reasoning behind training hard in specific actions towards specific threats so as to reduce the lag time created. This produces the required compression of time discussed by Boyd. Simplification has always been the most successful people's plan of action. Not only Boyd and Hick's, but also Rex Applegate and his proven philosophies of hand to hand combatives, knife fighting and shooting skills. They each rest upon the simplification of response techniques with speed and accuracy.

With visualization techniques, you are initiating motor programs. I have always preached the necessities

19

of mental planning for various situations. Whenever you are engaged with anyone, always preplan the event with the ideas of, "if they do this, I will respond with that." We are creating "known responses" to "known actions" and thus reducing lag time. Our fast response will cause them to pause so as to observe, orient, decide and then act. Their actions are stretching out time forcing them to fall further behind and thus incapable of overtaking you.

Boyd's diagram shows that the process is ever evolving, a fluid movement forward and re-initiating again with change. Every observation requires new orientation, decisions, and actions.

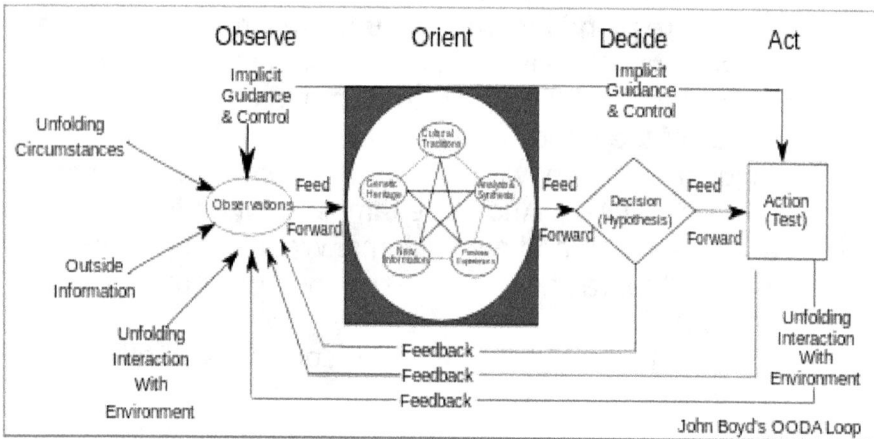

Diagram is from en.wikipedia.org

So how can the OODA loop principle be applied to law enforcement? Let's see how it is designed to win and then apply it to ourselves. Boyd said that in order to win, we should operate at a faster tempo than our adversaries or even better would be to get inside the adversary's OODA loop and disrupt their actions. This action can create confusion for an adversary causing them to stop their progression and react to yours.

The key is to obscure your intentions and make them unpredictable to your opponent while you simultaneously clarify his intentions. That is, operate at a faster tempo to generate rapidly changing conditions that inhibit your opponent from adapting or reacting to those changes and thus suppress or destroy their awareness. Therefore, confusion and disorder will occur and cause them to over- or under-react to your activities. You have to do something fast and unpredictable to keep them off guard and second guessing your actions.

Originally designed for the fighter pilot, Boyd's idea of the loop in action can be explained as a fighter pilot when you know an encounter with an enemy aircraft is imminent. Based on your intelligence you have to make a reasonable assumption of what type of aircraft and how trained is the pilot. As the enemy comes into radar range you determine speed, numbers and size. You decide to climb based on their altitude and approach with the sun at your back. This is the first completion of the loop. You observed, oriented, decided and acted. Now based on their reaction to your actions the loop repeats itself. How fast you can flow through the loop will be based upon your training and experience.

How does one interfere with an opponent's OODA cycle? One of Colonel Boyd's primary insights into fighter combat was that it is vital to change speed and direction faster than the opponent. This is not necessarily a function of the plane's ability to maneuver, rather the pilot must think and act faster than the opponent can think and act. To get "inside" the cycle—short-circuiting the opponent's thinking processes—produces opportunities for the opponent to react inappropriately.

At another level, an example could be that of a football player. A running back is handed the ball where he approaches a defensive player who is bigger and stronger. He knows he cannot simply run through him with much chance of success. Therefore, he slips aside and uses a series of short and fast body fakes which causes a moment of pause for the defensive player and eliminates his attributes of size and strength. Based on the running backs training and experience he takes advantage of the situation by accelerating past the opponent who over-reacts to his movements and slips by them. By taking advantage of the opponent's over-reaction to his fake, he has now broken the opponents loop and the opponent now has to react again based on the new parameters, but it will be too late as the running back goes past his position.

He has taken control of the situation by creating an advantage rather than reacting to the action. It is not simply a matter of moving through the loop faster, but most important is taking control of the situation. The OODA loop favors agility over raw power in dealing with human opponents in any endeavor. Boyd's practices created the idea of smaller and more agile fighter aircraft still in use today, the F16 and F18.

Now let's apply this theory to law enforcement. Most gun battles (81%) will occur in less than 21 feet. Almost 60% of them will occur at 5 feet or less. The most common method of public encounters is a traffic stop. You know that the preferred weapon of choice is a handgun or knife, especially at the common distances of a couple of feet. The subject is nervous and quickly reaches into his waistband and pulls a gun while stepping back. This is a difficult situation for the officer. If he stands there he will be shot or taken hostage. You will also be shot if you stand and try to draw your gun. Look at the loop. He has observed you, oriented by knowing he has been arrested multiple times in the past and will serve life if he is arrested again. He has decided to kill you rather than run away, and acted by drawing his gun. When you observed the action of him drawing the gun, you are at step one of the loop; observation. You still have to orient and decide on a course of action before acting on the decision. This can occur fast, but every second delayed is a second closer to death.

The only plausible action with any hope of success is to move laterally in the opposite side that the gun has been drawn. If they draw right handed, as 93% of the population will, your best course of action would be to run to your right while drawing your gun to return fire once a reasonable position has been reached. Your movement will cause them to re-initiate the loop to respond to your actions. With any luck at all, you can fire rapidly while moving and strike or disrupt their ability to shoot properly.

This has to be determined by a case by case scenario and using the above mentioned scene, both you and the bad guy are standing face to face. With the bad guy stepping back while drawing their weapon, you will not get to him in time to stop his action. Statistics show that you would have to be inside of 3 feet from the subject to effectively grab and try to overtake him. In the case of a traffic stop, a passenger's side approach is the safest and your first action upon seeing a weapon is to move to the rear of the car before drawing your weapon. This position provides you with cover and protection.

A better scenario is to keep the driver in their car. If they are outside with you, ask if they have ever been arrested. This is single question can save your life by heightening your awareness. Only 3% of offenders who assaulted and killed a police officer did not have any prior arrest. With this question you are already observing and can now move forward to orientation. Your previous experiences have told you that this person can be more dangerous. This causes your natural instincts of awareness to initiate. Now you also see that they are very nervous and starting to look around, all indications of the fight or flight scenario. They are observing and orienting as they try to decide the next best course of action. They are in step three of the loop. Remember, it is always better to get inside and disrupt their loop, thus short circuiting their thought process. You can initiate hands on or you can say, "Today is your lucky day. I have to let you go." This creates a break in their orienting phase which disrupts their decision before they act. Then you can seize them with an element of surprise or wait for back up to arrive.

Training and preparations for these situations are vital for their success. Remember Hick's Law and examine various events and situations that you will encounter based on your experiences and explore the best case scenario. When standing toe to toe interviewing a subject, say to yourself "If he tries to grab or hit me, I will instantly strike him in the throat." You are preparing your motor programs for an instantaneous response to their behavior. Should the subject grab or strike, rather than standing there stunned for a second, you will instantly respond. You are compressing the reactionary steps. With this preplanning and practice of your reactions to various scenarios, you are compressing time. When action is required, it will be instantaneous because you have already developed the mental and motor response of the actions. Otherwise, you will have to receive whatever they give as your mind decides the best course of action.

You have made a passenger's side approach on a vehicle and suddenly see a gun on the subject. Preplan that the safest response to this action is to run to the rear of the car and draw your weapon. It has been demonstrated that by trying to draw and run takes longer (too many options) than to first move to a safer zone and then draw your weapon. You mentally prepare and even practice this move several times. You think about the processes involved during each stop and passengers side approach. In the event that this description does occur, you are again compressing the time with a known response to a known action and dominating the scenario. To preplan will allow you to observe the gun, orient to the fact that there is a gun, decide what your best course of action will be and act. In this time frame you are delaying or creating a lag in your reactionary time, thus falling victim to their action.

You recognized their behaviors fast enough by paying attention. You interrupted their process thus gaining the advantage. In the first scenario, you were simply responding to their nearly completed action and placing yourself at a disadvantage. In the later examples you are rapidly responding to a known or anticipated action with a planned reaction which then places them at the disadvantage. It can almost classify as maneuver warfare by defeating an opponent by incapacitating their decision making by shock and disruption brought about by movement. It is one of two accepted practices of military theorist, a war of attrition or of movement. Movement is very effective when you are few, quick and fluid. Much greater armies have been defeated by an agile opponent. The same goes with law enforcement. In our gun scenario, lateral movement is critical. The same applies to an edged weapon. From a distance of 30 feet, an assailant can overtake and stab you by the time you recognize the threat, draw and shoot.. Again movement opposite their weapon creates or maintains distance and provides you with the time needed to bring your weapon into play. Also, it moves you to a direction away from their weapon. They have the additional movements needed of bringing the knife around to the opposite body side, thus a longer distance to hit.

Preplan and practice a fast movement to your right under these scenarios. We are playing the odds that 93% of the population is right handed. Your movement requires them to turn their entire body to respond to the action.

The last of this process is in understanding that once you begin, you have to continue until the threat is eliminated. As soon as you see them pulling a gun, instantly move and keep moving while drawing and firing continually. In the scenario of the traffic stop, move to the safe area, draw your weapon and be prepared to eliminate the threat. If they take no action, continue to move to the safety of your vehicle. Access and bring into the fight any long guns that you have available. In the other scenario where the subject physically assaults you, one strike to the throat may not be enough. Be prepared to take any action against them which will allow you the opportunity to separate. Use this separation to protect yourself with any additional weapons at your disposable. Their actions will dictate your level of force. It is not good enough to initiate a great plan and suddenly stop. Only consider stopping once you are no longer in danger.

Fatal Errors and Flaws

5

Over here, over there, everywhere,

Today, tomorrow, always:

Bad men there are.

Hate you they do.

Kill you they will.

Watch out you better.

- Old Shoshone Refrain

I have always mentioned the Fatal Errors and everyone has seen them many times during training. However, it is apparent that no one has retained the information that these simple commandments, if you will, express. Nearly all of them deal within the realm of mental planning and preparations. Like most actions in life, police work or shall I say effective and safe police work, is mental. When we lose focus and attention, we get hurt and killed. Add to this the fact that police work is the most stressful job in the civilized world, mental planning is everything. Let's look at the ten most common Fatal Errors. I will place "physical" or "mental" at the end of each to denote if this category is a physical or mental task.

1. **Attitude** – This does not indicate our projected attitude that people see such as, anger, happy, aggressive, etc. This is the title given to attention failure. Attention is one of the most important mental states we possess and is why attention is Chapter 6 by itself. It affects almost everything we do. Understanding how to control your attention is paramount to safety. We will fail ourselves, our families, and the citizens we protect by a lack of proper attitude. This is how we mentally prepare ourselves to face the day. Are we going to focus on the task as they occur or fail to keep our head in the game? Are we going to let uncontrollable events affect the way we approach our job? Things like: no pay raise again, my supervisor sucks, my kid failed a class, my wife lost her job, or my air conditioning broke. Any and all of these can affect your attitude, creating distractions and blocking your ability to "see" the dangers when they approach. The number one rule of law enforcement has always been and will always be, to come home safe at the end of your shift. **"Mental"**

2. **Tombstone Courage** – This is known as the "John Wayne" effect. It's an approach that dates back as far as law enforcement. I wear a badge and carry a gun. I possess the authority to enforce the law. I will be respected and obeyed. This may have been true in centuries past, but times, society and parenting have changed. Children are taught to resist authority and it shows. The family has broken down and with it the necessary nurturing from two parents to instill moral and family values in their children. Respect is given to the bad guys more often than law enforcement. No one believes they have ever done anything wrong; the parents support the children over the school and the judicial system. Once tragedy occurs they will complain that everyone, except for themselves, has let this child down. Respect for your position, as anyone who has worked the streets for any time will attest, fades further each year. Everyone wants to argue, has an excuse, feels profiled, or thinks they are innocent. We understand the dangers involved. I

even explained in my previous books how the streets of America can be more dangerous than the battlefields of Iraq and Afghanistan. The days of the "One Riot, One Ranger" philosophy is gone. Wait for back up when taking police actions which could lead to a detention. **"Mental"**

3. Rest – This one topic is considered by most research today as the most important of the errors. There is no replacement for the necessary hours of sleep on your performance. Force Science Research has shown that police officers who do not get the necessary sleep each night have various medical problems and dangers associated with this simple process. Athletes have been shown the three necessities of a successful career; proper diet, sleep (at least 8 hours each day), and exercise. No single one of these is any more important than the other. Failure to accomplish one and the entire process fails. After a 2 year sleep study involving 5000 officers, 46% had nodded off while driving, 40% had sleep disorders and 53.9% of the night shift had improper sleep habits and insomnia. Officers with sleep disorders were twice as likely to experience events in their career with negative consequences. Though 94% considered themselves in good physical shape, 79% were overweight. Lack of sleep had adverse effects on decision making and performance. You are a warrior. The proof is in the statistics. Warriors fight, get injured, and sometimes killed for the cause they believe in. Few mourn your loss more than your fellow warriors. It is a simple solution to a simple problem. **"Mental"**

4. Bad Positioning – Good situational awareness techniques will assist you in proper positioning tactics based on the type of action involved. There are many various observations needed in an encounter. Notice any changes in behaviors, consciously exercise your mental planning and tactics, always place yourself in a position of advantage, and have good situational awareness skills. When you make traffic stops, observe their pre and post stop behaviors, watch for the critical issues like brake lights and turn signals. Stop your car at least two car lengths back, keep everyone in their car and approach on the passenger's side if possible. When backing up another officer, determine the situation and position yourself to cover the occupants while not becoming involved with the stop. If you are involved in a foot pursuit, follow the proper tactics to always maintain a position of safety. Everything we do involves positioning and situational awareness of the environment. Be sure to follow these simple rules. **"Mental"**

5. Recognizing Danger – This is the attention and recognition of the critical issues that are presented each time you come across someone. I can assure you that someone on a regular basis has considered harming you during your shift. Take the initiative to follow the maxim I proposed in *Tactical Survival* of Study Train Survive. Study the intricacies of the job and always learn the newest tactics and techniques through training. They have the advantage of surprise in their favor and action almost always beats reaction. Utilizing attention with training and experience can give you precious seconds with advance recognition of a behavior. This allows you to move to the all-important phase 2 or time compression of the OODA loop. Your next actions can have lifelong consequences. Understanding these philosophies and the reactions to them can increase your survival odds. **"Mental"**

6. Hands – These are the two primary body parts of the suspects which will hurt you. Know where they are and what is in them at every second of your encounter. 16,000 officers will be assaulted and injured each year and it is in your best interest to try and not be one of those victim officers. How do you do that? There is a multitude of answers that I am trying to answer in all of my books. We are studying behaviors and reactions to those behaviors. I will repeat this phrase numerous times, but action always beats reaction. If you know from where the assault will initiate, then you have to make a conscious effort to keep track of their hands. Never let them reach into a pocket, stand with their arms behind them, approach a car without being able to see them or become involved with anyone without their hands in plain sight. The FBI has reported that this single action of keeping their hands in sight can greatly reduce the chances of the officer being killed. There are some of you reading this and saying "this is common sense." It is common sense, but is also a common error repeated by everyone each day as we allow our attention to be diverted. **"Mental"**

7. Relaxing Too Soon – Another word for this is complacency and we have already discussed how it occurs. Never trust the person encountered. Un-events will occur on a regular basis. What I mean is that each and every day many of the things that we do, begin to seem routine. As these un-events fail to unfold anything new, we start to perceive this state as normal. Later in this chapter, it will be explained in detail as the Normalization of Deviance. We begin taking short cuts. We feel over confident on our experiences and believe we will recognize an event before it can happen. The truth of the matter is that we must maintain a consistency in the way we conduct ourselves with nearly everyone. This helps to prevent the shortcuts. Relaxing too soon is taking a short cut. We know we cannot afford to play catch up as action always beats reaction. Relax after the encounter. You can never let your guard down when dealing with the public. **"Mental"**

8. Handcuffing – This is usually the lack of handcuffing or poor handcuffing tactics. You can always take them off later, but if you are suspicious enough to detain them, handcuff them. It eliminates the threat of number 6, the hands. It is not only important to handcuff the suspect, but you must properly handcuff them. We have all heard about someone escaping an officer's custody by slipping out of the handcuffs. It occurs more often than we like to imagine. Again, what we are talking about is taking a short cut. Secure them with their hands behind the back, palms out, tight enough to prevent them from slipping out, and double lock the cuffs. Many of you will read this and say, "This is the basics we learned on the first day!" True, oh so very true. However, each day we work without an incident the un-events begin to feel normal. Ignore all of the complaining from the suspects about the cuffs. They were never intended to be comfortable. Pay attention to the basics. **"Mental"**

9. Search – When the conditions are correct and safe, conduct a search. If there is a need to search and not just a quick pat down, remember number 8, handcuffing. Everyone will miss something in a search at some point in their career. We have to take our time and be methodical. Start and finish at the same place each time. Make it a habit to be thorough. Many of us have been killed because we failed this simple task. Never assume someone else conducted a thorough search. Search them again if you are transporting for another officer. This is also the place to bring up search locations of persons. The bad guys know that we will not thoroughly search females and usually fail to conduct a great search on men. They will hide weapons and contraband in the one area most frequently overlooked the crotch. In fact, 75% of criminals will hide their articles of contraband in the crotch because they state that they have either never been searched there or not very well searched. In men arrestees, you have to thoroughly grab all of the area to see if there are more objects in place than are supposed to be there. For female arrestees, male officers are getting away from the basics out of fear of complaints. Run the back of your hand around their waist and pockets to ensure that there is nothing immediately available. Have a female officer conduct a thorough search later if they are arrested. Explain to them that they will be strip searched at the jail facility and if they have anything on them, it will result in additional charges. Also, search the rear of your car each and every time anyone is placed there to ensure anything found can be charged to the current suspect. They may be afraid to tell you they have something secreted and remove it in the rear of your car. **"Mental"**

10. Equipment – Be proficient with your equipment and understand the need for back up gear for your primary tools. Keep a basic survival rule of our Special Operations Forces; 2 is 1, 1 is none. If your primary equipment fails and you do not have a backup, it is the same as not having anything at all. A gun that fails when it's needed or a flashlight dies when lighting is critical jeopardizes your survival. Carry a backup weapon, two flashlights, two knives, multiple handcuff keys, and a go-bag in the trunk of your car. In the bag you can carry a change of clothing including boots, snacks and a camelback or bottled water. Never allow this simple action to endanger you or prevent you from continuing your work when needed. **"Mental"**

In addition to the "Fatal Errors" committed by law enforcement, another area of review conducted by the FBI was the "Fatal Flaws." These are the areas determined by the researchers to be the primary mistakes committed by the officers which led to their deaths. After the completion of each three part study the FBI maintained a Fatal Flaws list. After 15 years and the completion of the study, the list remained the same. The reason is we rarely change our training modules and believe we would never commit them. Each and every one of these mistakes is directly contributable to failed mental planning. In both of my previous books, *Criminal Interdiction* and *Tactical Survival,* I have discussed these issues. Understanding how vital they are is essential.

1. Failure to wait for back up. This is the number one reason in my opinion why we are continually killed and injured on the job. There is this false impression that everyone will respond to your lawful commands and authority. The truth is nowhere near this belief. At the time of arrest, they are on equal ground with you. This is the time to expect things to go wrong. I know we have all arrested people without incident while alone or had them flee after passive resistance. Sooner or later, you will find the one person who knows they have multiple previous arrests and are facing enhanced prison time who will aggressively assault you in an effort to escape the situation. Wait for backup whenever it is at all possible.

2. The failure to draw your weapon when the situation called for it. Too many of us have had the "best interest of the department" pounded into our psyche, especially from inside the training academies. There are many agencies that have gone too far to the left with their political correctness ideas and call the display of your firearm in the performance of duties as a "use of force." This is in my opinion a "show of force." The more it is pounded into your mind that every time you draw your weapon it equates to a negative act, your life is being placed in greater jeopardy. It becomes a Normalization of Deviance and creating a negative impression in your mind. This short circuiting of an essential action creates a lag in your response time and ultimately endangers your life. If the situation calls for it, draw your weapon. This simple action is moving you forward into the OODA loop and better preparing you to meet the possible threat.

3. Tunnel vision when dealing with more than one suspect. This is another common mistake by law enforcement. It deals with the concept of attention redirection. If it is at all possible, we should always try to avoid dealing with multiple persons without backup. It is simply impossible to properly cover more than one person if you are alone. Remember, if you are a cover officer, it is your job to only be a cover officer. It is required that you stay back to oversee the entire scene and not become involved at all with any facet of the investigation unless it is required. The tactics of the cover officer will be discussed in the next chapter. For this topic, peripheral vision is explained. Peripheral vision is a part of vision that occurs outside the very center of gaze. It is utilized for detecting motion. The loss of peripheral vision, while retaining central vision is known as tunnel vision. In other words, our peripheral vision is designed to recognize motion that occurs around us. In a stressful event, all focus is placed on the center of gaze, thus giving us tunnel vision. This bodily response to stress also places us in grave danger when dealing with more than one person. We will never see the others begin to move toward us from a flanking position.

4. Failure to keep people in their cars. This is again an issue of the previous scenarios. Once a person is allowed to exit their car, they are on equal footing with you. Equality is not a logical feature of this scenario. The advantage must always be with the officer. If more than one person exits a car, there are the dangers of tunnel vision. Without a cover officer, you are at a disadvantage.

5. Proper vehicle placement after a traffic stop.
Proper vehicle placement after a traffic stop carries with it a double front line of protection. First, most officers will correlate the positioning from the threat that could exist from within the car. The second threat is from the approaching traffic from behind. This is a very critical consideration because statistics show that more than 50% of all police officer deaths have a traffic component. First of all, when conducting a traffic stop, you should stop at least 2 car lengths back if possible, from the target vehicle. In addition, you should pull as far off the road as is reasonable. This helps you against both threats. If the subject was to exit the car with a firearm, you have allowed yourself some distance to provide a reaction. Second if your car is struck from behind, this distance allows absorption of energy. It will also reduce the impact to the violator's vehicle which provides you additional protection from the energy of the striking car.

6. Failure to immediately control a known suspect.
This is directly attached to number 8 in the Fatal Errors category of "Handcuffing". If you have a known or even a suspect of a crime, it is essential to your safety to control the two body parts that can cause harm; the hands. As I said before, if you can legally detain them, handcuff their hands behind their back, palms out.

7. Mental planning of different scenarios. I have talked about the importance of this this topic in terms of the OODA Loop, Hick's Law, and Rex Applegate's training. There are those in the field today who will say that visualization techniques do nothing. Yet, everyone in the business of self-defense, law enforcement, athletics and combatives can all explain how effective mental planning is to any scenario.

Again I believe that it all falls back to what is known as, "The Normalization of Deviance." This is a term developed by NASA and former shuttle commander Dr. Story Musgrove after investigating what happened to the Challenger and Columbia Space Shuttles. NASA had identified both of these failures on previous missions. The degradation of the O-rings on the Challenger shuttle had been noted on prior missions. The powers to be were notified by the manufacturer that they could get worse in cold weather.

Minor tile damage had become common and expected after shuttle take offs. In both cases, NASA had determined the damage as "acceptable." With each successful mission, the acceptability of problems (quality control) worsened because nothing negative had ever happened. Sadly, as with most things in our lives, there are no compliance without consequence.

The Normalization of Deviance is the downward change in standards each time a successful mission is completed, even with the forewarned knowledge of trouble. This is a condition which applies to all areas of human existence including law enforcement. Each time we rush through or take short cuts in the processes, we mentally cause deviations in our thinking. "I am able to do this without ever doing that and nothing ever happens to me." It creates "acceptable" dangers in a profession where there can be none. It is a simple process of mental concentrations to the processes we have been taught which we know will work. Eventually, the short cuts will lead you down a very slippery trail; One that can cost you your life.

Another important cluster of facts can also play out in regards to all of this information. During the FBI's 15 year study they also looked at the officers and their personality/ behavior traits. It was discovered that each of the 54 murdered officers in the study carried at least two (2) or more of the descriptive traits as described by not only the officers who knew them, but from the assailant who murdered them. Here is the list:

- Friendly to everyone
- Well-liked by community and department
- Tends to use less force than other officers felt they would in similar situations
- Hard working
- Tends to perceive self as more public relations than law enforcement or very service oriented
- Use force only as a last resort – peers claim they would use force at an earlier point in similar circumstances
- Doesn't follow all of the rules, especially in regard to:
  Arrest
  Confrontation with prisoners
  Traffic stops
  Does not wait for backup
- Feels they can "read" others/situations and will drop guard as a result
- Tends to look for "good" in others
- "Laid back" and "easy going"

What we see is a combination of many of the areas of concern I have wrote about previously. Not waiting for back up, being too friendly, not recognizing /

reacting to dangers, and taking short cuts. Often time's police are seen as rude, rough, and mean. There are times for "Officer Friendly" to be displayed. You cannot in every occurrence be hard. Common sense, an attribute which is so often lacking, has to come into each scenario. Each time you encounter someone in a traffic stop for instance, you do not have to be a machine. You can be firm when needed yet remember this is not a social call, it is a traffic stop. Your attitude should be displayed as stern and serious by appearance or presence only. If you stop a mother with her children or an elderly couple you can still be polite and firm.

Unfortunately, many agencies and supervisors do not understand that this is a job of confrontation. Complaints will be made against everyone at some point. It is the job of the supervisor to handle these issues, but many see it as just more paperwork and chastise the officer. Many of the "mottos" can themselves lead to unrealistic expectations from people who have not worked the street for years and civilians alike. "Courtesy, Service, and Protection" gets mixed with departmental attitudes of "Officer Friendly." This consistent laid back attitude of many officers raises the odds against you. Society changes on a regular basis and continually becomes more violent. Do the job with your safety as the principal issue each day. Follow the rules as you have been taught and continue to learn. Together you will raise the odds in your favor should one day evil approaches with a smile on their face.

Attention

-moral ambiguity is what the threat counts on during the initial phase of his assault, to delay your appropriate response just long enough to kill you.

- Mike Straw

If you read this chapter and parts of it appears familiar, that is because it is from my book, *Tactical Survival*. I spoke at length about the importance of attention to the safety of a police officer. I have included it again as a refresher with additional information on the Colavita Dominance effect. This is an important scientifically proven event which occurs in all of us. Recently, the Colavita Dominance theory was brought into a trial in California as a cause and affect involving a police shooting event. Attention plays a vital role in maintaining the correct mental focus to avoid all of the negatives from the last chapter.

I included these topics together because you cannot read one without being aware of the others. We know about learning to read body languages, voice commands, and responses (all of which I will discuss), but attention? Attention or our attention to detail is an important aspect of officer safety. Attention is how the brain operates when receiving the information from our surrounding environment through all of the various sensory receptions. Think about the various mental distractions we have to work with each day. However, our brains can only focus its attention on one thing at a time. It will remove all other issues from your attention span to focus on that issue.

Despite how good we think we are at multitasking, we are really only good at one thing at a time. When we think we are multitasking, our minds are actually switching from one activity to the other. There are many who believe they are excellent at multitasking. You can drive, watch the calls on the computer screen, listen to the patrol radio, and talk on the cell phone. In reality, your brain is only programmed to handle one of these situations at a time. When you are involved in one, the others are not getting any attention. You say to yourself, "but I am on the phone all of the time and driving while watching the calls on the computer." Yes you are, just not at the same time. Think back to when you were trying to read the notes on the computer and talking to someone on the cell phone. One or the other actually gets cut off for that moment as you switch your attention between the two. Then suddenly, you brake hard to avoid a collision because your attention to driving was also turned off. When we have been driving for many years, the actions we take are more reactionary. You do not have to think about when to brake, accelerate, or turn the steering wheel. They are simply trained motor skills. Accidents occur when you do not notice to take the action in time.

The brain is unable to focus on everything so it tries to prioritize the most important. What it considers important at that moment may not be the most significant thing to you. Additionally, thinking about other issues in your life will lead to an inability to focus. Attention is like a spotlight and you will only notice the objects in the light. If you spotlight on one person, no one else will be noticed. This is the inherent danger of dealing with multiple suspects. When they are out of the car or as pedestrians, you cannot deal with them all.

As we enter the topic of attention focus, let me explain how the eyes work in conjunction with the brain. The entire eye is designed to track motion. We have 2 types of eyesight, central and peripheral. The central is the eye sight which is directly in front of us. The peripheral is the sight zone to the sides of the center. The central sight zone observes more than the peripherals. The peripheral sights are not as strong and capable of recognizing only one movement at a time. This movement recognition is for faster motion. In other words, if two movements of various speeds occur in your peripheral zone, the faster moving object will be observed while other movements can be missed. Keep this concept in mind as we explore the upcoming topics of attention and redirection. Understanding why a process works will explain the outcome of the event.

Keep everyone in their cars until a situation arises that requires them to be out. Try not to deal with multiple suspects until you have backup. Without standing back to take in the entire event, you cannot handle them safely. If you must take action, separate one and make the others stay away. As additional officers arrive on the scene, direct them to focus on the others. Recently, in central Florida, an officer was shot in the head and killed while patting down three suspicious subjects. He knew back up was on the way and failed to wait. We have all done this same thing many times before in our careers. This is NOT criticism of this fallen officer. It is a harsh lessens for the rest of us. When trying to do multiple things when dealing with a suspect, you will only do one thing right. This one thing will then be something else, then something else, and so on. If you will remember this simple fact of attention it may one day pay off in saving your life. Remember the FBI statistics that 38% of officers were killed during a crime in progress. 60% of those officers were killed while trying to make an arrest of the suspect before backup had arrived.

Attention can be controlled by distraction or misdirection. One person could start going through their wallet, which will focus your attention. The other suspect recognizes that you are concentrating on the item and pulls a weapon or discards contraband. If focused on a specific item or subject, you may not recognize the developing dangers.

In order to prevent this, stand back and control the encounter. Do not move close and wait for back up. By standing back and not focusing attention to a single person or object, you are keeping your attention on the entire chain of events. The moment you start reading driver's licenses or writing notes, your attention is now misdirected from the overall situation. Make sure they keep their hands out of pockets and in sight.

This brings up a fascinating reality called inattentional blindness. The brain is simply too overwhelmed with everything in our environment. Therefore, we developed attention to keep us focused on specific items of interest. Remember that we can only focus on a single event. To allow this to happen, our brain ignores everything else. Because of this normal psychological event, large things can occur around us and we never see it happen. Think of magicians when they have you concentrating on one thing while changes occur in the background. They are not expected and your focus is directed; therefore, you will not notice it. You may not always recognize change where it is not expected. This is a common cause of motorcycle accidents. We look down the road before pulling out from a side street. We take a quick glance. Our mind is focused on cars, vans, trucks, etc. A motorcycle, bicyclist, or pedestrian approaching is literally removed from the vision. An accident occurs and we are left telling everyone, "I looked and never saw anything. I have no idea where they came from."

The same psychology applies to law enforcement. Knowing how this "change blindness" occurs, train yourself to focus on a series of events. For instance, you are about to stop a car. Training teaches us to watch the people inside the car and their behaviors such as: how the driver operates the car, where the driver is looking, the brake lights and turn signals, how they pull off of the road and stop their vehicle. Can you pay attention to all of these things at once? From a distance, your center of attention is the car. As you focus on more specifics, create a checklist of things before, during, and after the stop. If you follow this checklist of indicators, then one by one, eliminate them from the list. You catch up to the car and do not immediately activate your emergency equipment. You observe the driver and passengers. How are they behaving? Is the driver watching you in the side and rear view mirrors? What about the car, is the license plate proper? Now is the time to run the tag, not after the stop. Are there air fresheners, bumper stickers, rental car signs, or other things that could heighten the event?

In your mind you have check listed the occupants and the car itself. Initiate the emergency equipment and proceed with the traffic stop. Does the car stop in a reasonable manner or travel some distance before stopping? What are the occupants doing? Did the car stop a safe distance from the road? Are you stopping about two car lengths back from them? Are the brake lights and/or turn signals still activated?

You can see how placing the item into a mental checklist allows you to safely conduct the stop. Most officers will observe the car and make the stop. They may notice a couple of the items, yet miss many more. There are just too many things to pay attention too at the same time. The ones missed could be the signal needed to save your life.

Attention redirection is an action we use more often without realizing. A pick pocket artist will be good at redirecting your attention. They get you to look at one thing while they concentrate on taking something else. Magicians and illusionist do the same thing. "Watch the cards," they will say which focuses your attention. Once that has happened, they can do most anything else they want. Keep in mind that attention is single topic focused. If your focus is where someone does not want it to be, they will cause a distraction to redirect your attention. Remember the Lunsford tape out of Texas? He has two subjects out of the car while searching the trunk. There is no way to see everything they are doing. They distracted and then rushed him. In the first chapter of this book we see another example of attention redirection. Bart Johnson tells Officer Davis about his brother the police officer. Officer Davis reaches for a notepad from his pocket which opened the door of opportunity for Johnson to shoot him. An attention redirection was added which caused the officer to be distracted

Suspect behaviors tell all if you can maintain your attention to the details like developing a baseline. You've experienced hundreds of different people during the course of your job and developed a baseline for normal behaviors. When you come across someone behaving completely different, focus on them and investigate the reasons for the mannerisms. It can be compared to animal behaviors. Domesticated animals like to interact with people. They are curious and trusting. Wild animals never want to get close to humans. They are not curious and live in a constant state of fright, flight or fight. Given the chance they will leave. Left with no options, they will fight. This is the same with criminals and the average person. Normal people have no problem being around you while the crook wants to stay away.

The limbic system is a set of brain structures which support a variety of functions including emotion, behavior, motivation, long term memory, and olfaction. When you are observing people, constantly search for overt behavior displayed due to nervous emotions and feelings. When someone is nervous, the limbic system in the brain will recognize that stressor and begin to generate energy that will be used in the fright, flight or fight response that follows.

I've talked about this topic in every class and book. Body language or Kinesics is the study of nonlinguistic body movements. We all have behaviors that will exaggerate under pressure. Just as a polygraph machine measures changes in blood pressure and heart rate, so can you. These changes cause a person to sweat and adjust behaviors. Start watching everyone's behaviors when you have them stopped. Pay attention to their breathing, their pulse rate in the neck, the pulse in their suprasternal notch, their hands and what they do with them. The standard for a resting heart rate is 60 – 100 beats per minute. If you are out with someone and you have back up present, ask them if you can check their heart rate. Check the brachial pulse in their arm, or if they say no, simply watch the pulse rate in their neck. Count the number of beats in 10 seconds and multiply that by 6. This will give you an approximate heart rate which will help you to determine how stressed they are.

Do their hands shake, but relax as the encounter progresses? This shows how they are calming down in your presence and therefore not feeling guilty. Pay attention as they fumble through their wallets and purses. Do they tremble, try to hide the contents, or start to look and then stop to say they cannot find what you have asked them for? Pay attention to their eye movements and the direction they are looking. They will often seek a way out or towards your weapons, their car, their accomplices, etc. Observe their inability to stand still while asking them questions. Make a mental note of the items in plain view around them. They can tell a lot about the habits of the person. Is there Visine or lighters in the console or seat next to them? Ask them if they smoke. People keep close the things they use regularly. Why have a lighter immediately available if you do not smoke? Chapter 9 of *Criminal Interdiction* is dedicated to this topic.

There is one behavior which I believe is the single most important an officer can pay attention to; audio occlusion. When you repeat your commands, be prepared. Command repetition occurs when the person is beginning to shut you out because their mind is becoming occupied. This is an ideal time to discuss the Colavita Visual Dominance effect. This phenomenon is best described as whenever you have two separate stimuli of a visual and auditory nature, the brain automatically overrides towards the visual. In other words, a suspect you stop is stressed. You are giving him verbal commands. His visual channels will override the auditory and he will fail to hear you. A visual can be internalization as well when they are trying to decide their next course of action. They will never hear your complete sentences and fail to obey your commands. They are redirecting their focus internally and we can only direct our attention on one thing at a time. The internal thought processes are unlikely for anyone confronted by the police. They are entering their fight or flight, over stressed, adrenaline pump. They are very scared and are mentally trying to decide the best course of action for themselves. In almost every video of an officer being assaulted or killed, you will hear the officer repeat themselves to the suspect at some point before the attack. It may occur only once, but you will clearly see the behavioral change of the suspect. Just as you are paying attention to the video, pay attention to your suspects. Avoid distractions because this is when they will initiate their actions.

Situational awareness is a topic we need to be reminded of to keep it in the forefront of our minds. You are taking stock in your surrounding environment. You have to be aware of the areas and the people in them. When stopped and writing reports, be cognizant of the area you park, the accesses and blind spots, as well as looking around frequently for anyone approaching. The largest, empty lot makes a good place to park so you can see 360 degrees around. Do not wear your seat belt to allow for a quick exit if needed. Several officers are killed each year from having someone approach and shoot them while they are sitting in their cars. Apply the same precautions while in restaurants or other businesses. How often have you seen the events of a deranged gunman entering a restaurant or other establishment and start shooting everyone? Sadly, it is a common occurrence around the world. Remember that there were three police officers murdered in 2011 as they sat in their cars while not involved in any specific police duty. They were simply in uniform and presented a target.

In *Criminal Interdiction,* I described situational awareness as:
"Be aware of your surroundings at all times. I already know that this not completely possible all of the time. But just like your traffic stops, everywhere you stop should be considered. As you pull into a parking lot or an

abandoned area to work on reports, be aware of the area. When walking into restaurants or convenience stores, do you survey what is going on inside before entering? Do you sit at a restaurant in a place of advantage or disadvantage? Wild Bill Hickok was killed while sitting at a table with his back to a door. Recently in Washington State, four police officers were shot to death while sitting at a table and working on their computers at a coffee shop. Situational awareness is everywhere you go on or off duty. You should park in an area where you can leave easily and is well lit. The area where you park should have a clear view all around. This is so you will not be surprised if someone approaches you. Remember, with the technologies that exist today in a patrol car, like in car computers, it causes us to stare at the technology all of the time. Be aware of your surroundings at all times."

Situational awareness is ever changing, fluid and is difficult at best to maintain for very long. At home and in our personal lives, we can relax. Constantly being aware can cause a person to breakdown over time. Our lifestyles have given us a tendency to allow a daily routine to govern our lives. During routines, no or little thought has to occur. Everything just "is," as it flows in and out of our experiences. It becomes easy to allow this calm or routine to flow into our work. Repetition without failure creates a sense of normalcy. As was described in Chapter 5, The Normalization of Deviance begins to overcome the areas which we know to avoid, yet do not.

Sports psychologist and top Olympic coaches use visualization techniques for their athletes. It is estimated that 90% of Olympic athletes use some form of visualization and 97% say it helps. Visualization techniques can also reduce stresses and builds confidence. It helps you to focus on doing important things right and is proven to help when the actual task is performed. The mental imaging initiates the repetitive muscle responses which will place the action into your normal motor skills. You can see why this simple mind practice can make a difference in your survival.

When alone, you should practice visualization techniques involving various scenarios. Have them in mind during a traffic stop or other types of encounters. Quickly say in your mind, "If this person does A, I will respond with B. I can follow B with C and D if necessary." These brain games will prepare your mind for various types of threatening events which can occur. Therefore, if they happen, you will automatically respond with planned motor skills. This instant reaction can mean the difference for your survival.

Maintain mental awareness regardless of your agencies actions. What I mean is this is a job of offensive measures despite what your department's political correctness advocates. Job safety depends upon your swift decisions and actions to problems. A good cop is one who is aggressive. They seek out the criminals, not wait for the next call to come in from a civilian. Do not fall into a defensive mindset. Maintain the offensive and take the fight to them.

Agencies bowing down to public opinions based upon political correctness have hurt and killed officers. We do not have to wait for suspects to hit, kick, grab, resist, stab, try to run over, or even shoot before you take action. This entire idea of defensive tactics is ridiculous when you consider that our job is to restrain and arrest which can only be accomplished through offensive tactics. To protect life and property does not mean to sit and wait for them to take the first action. Take the initiative or offense to keep yourself safe.

In 2011 there were four officers and 8 in 2012 killed in ambush style attacks by gunfire. Many more were ambushed and not killed. You have to remember that this world is a dangerous place. Your destiny will be equivalent to how well you are prepared. Not all evils can be prevented, but situational awareness and visualization techniques can help.

Preparations

7

Martyrs alert the world to the presence of evil. Warriors do something about it.

- Phil Messina

Once we have directed ourselves towards self-observations of attention understanding, we can now apply it to behaviors. Observation and recognition of behaviors is the difference of survival in a deadly encounter. Advance recognition of their behaviors has taken you through phase 2 of the OODA loop which can be a second faster than someone else. In a life threatening battle, a few seconds is everything. We also discussed the importance of avoiding distractions. Distractions are intentional acts to draw you away from the focus of the events. This is the reasoning behind the refresher chapter of attention. Simple distractions have led to the deaths and injuries of many police officers over the decades. Understanding how to avoid them is imperative. Recently, I watched a video of an officer who arrests the driver of a car. A female passenger is allowed to roam around on the scene. A second passenger is in the car and a backup officer arrives at the scene. Remember the role of a backup or cover officer. They are only there to cover you. They are not to engage in the activities unless the situation escalates and are needed. Because of the pacing and talkative female, the cover officer is now completely engaged with her. His role has changed because he allowed it. The rear seat passenger pulls a gun and the original officer is eventually killed. Learn how to avoid distractions, recognize behaviors, and control the scenes.

It has been long understood that only through proper preparations can we have the highest expectations of success. Throughout time, soldiers, philosophers, and sports figures have described preparation in various forms.

- "In the fields of observation, chance favors only the prepared mind." – Louis Pasteur
- "We do not rise to the level of our expectations; we fall to the level of our training." – Archilochus
- "Pressure is something that you feel only when you don't know what you're doing." – Chuck Knoll
- "The cerebral part of the game is the most challenging part of the game. The cerebral part is where you can advance yourself and (what you) have to constantly stay on top of. I think sometimes you can get away with the physical part with being a great athlete. I can overcome that, but the cerebral part, you can't get behind in the mental aspect of the game. Everything happens so fast." – Peyton Manning
- "Success depends upon previous preparation, and without such preparation there is sure to be failure." – Confucius
- "Luck is what happens when preparation meets opportunity." - Seneca
- "There are no secrets to success. It is the result of preparation, hard work, and learning from failure." – Colin Powell

Preparations can carry with it a multitude of meaning. We should understand that physical fitness is a process to follow for general health. We also discovered that our appearance can have a significant importance to our safety. The FBI study of interviewed cop killers discovered that many of the murdered officers died as a result of their appearance. They were sloppy, overweight, and practiced poor safety procedures. The bad guy knew they could overcome them so like any predator, did.

We also learned that stress is the primary cause of many of the ill's that plague law enforcement. Heart attacks are a yearly event which leads to many officers deaths. There were 9 in 2011while on duty and countless more off duty. Physical fitness and diet control has to be placed high in the order of necessary preparations for law enforcement. It also plays a critical role in a Force Science research study. In their force Fatigue Threshold study, they measure how it takes before the body begins to lose energy to maintain the fight. The study utilized officers who considered themselves fit. The conclusions of the study showed that he body begins to lose strength within 30 seconds and within 2 minutes, the upper body is fatigued. It takes the body an amazing 15 minutes to recover from the event and more energy is utilized to restrain than resist. Therefore, if you decide to fight someone of equal strengths, the advantage is still theirs as you try to restrain them. These numbers will be reduced, in some cases drastically, based upon your own physical conditioning, weather, and the amount of equipment you are carrying. The FBI found in one of their studies that 12% of the murdered officers who went to the ground in a fight died by one of their own weapons. In my opinion, this study explains this statistic. Within 2 minutes your upper body has fatigued. No longer capable of defending yourself, the bag guy removes a weapon and kills you. You would not imagine going to work without a service weapon; you should never go to work unfit either mentally or physically.

Of equal importance and in many cases of a far greater importance, are the preparations of the mind. As seen earlier, the mental aspects of the job creates most of the life threatening incidences. We need to fully understand our own focus abilities and strive every day to enhance them. I suggested in *Tactical Survival,* one way to help us maintain control of our attention is through a mental checklist before an actual encounter takes place.

By doing this, we can assure ourselves of covering many of the pertinent areas of the event.

According to the Academy of Achievement, a Washington based group designed to bring together the world's most successful people with successful students, there are six keys to success.

1. Passion – A strong feeling or emotion. This career requires passion. You must have a deep passion to overcome evil. Police officers are America's soldiers at home. Without passion in your heart for the job you are simply taking up space. "The inner drive that turns your dreams into a shining reality."

2. Vision – A vivid mental image. "To attain your goal, you must first see it in your mental eye." Just as I have been preaching all along, it is in our mindset that all things will be achieved. If you allow distractions to enter your mindset at the critical moments, one day a consequence will befall.

3. Preparation - The cognitive process of thinking about what you will do if something happens. "Success isn't a matter of luck- it requires practice, study and strategy." We see it in the famous quote mentioned above by Seneca; "Luck is what happens when preparation meets opportunity." Look at the definition itself. You must prepare yourself to overcome adversity. Preparation equates to training. It lies within my own maxim from *Tactical Survival,* Study Train Survive.

4. Courage - A quality of spirit that enables you to face danger. The ability to "prevail despite hardship, pain and mortal danger." I have always proclaimed to all that it takes a special person to become a police officer and an even greater person to dedicate your life to the profession. Just as most soldiers stay in the services for only a few years, so will most police officers. Then there are those who become "lifers" in both the domestic and foreign services.

5. Perseverance – This stands for not just determination, but for persistent determination. "No great achievement comes without obstacles." Although they were met with failure, they "doggedly persevered until they succeeded against the odds." Regardless of the situation, you represent justice in our society despite what a minority of the population is led to believe. With the correct training and practice you can overcome even the worst of situations.
6. Integrity – An undivided completeness with nothing wanting. A moral soundness. "The road that leads to real success has no short cuts." (Normalization of Deviance) It is an internal awareness that separates you from most others. It establishes trust which without; you become the antithesis of what you stand for.

Imagine a profession that is founded upon these principles. At the Academy of Achievement, the greatest and most successful people are brought together with some of this country's brightest students. These students are taught that to reach the level of their mentors which range from former presidents, military generals, and athletes, these are the six categories of understanding for achievement. They are ours as well. Smile when you understand that these same principles have been our foundation since the first people, afraid of the evil within the populace, hired someone for protection.

Representational Channels

8

He that has eyes to see and ears to hear may convince himself that no mortal can keep a secret. If his lips are silent, he chatters with his fingertips; betrayal oozes out of him at every pore.

- Sigmund Freud

Communication or informational exchanges pass to and from us via 3 Representational Channels or modalities by which we communicate. These Channels are Visual, Auditory, and Internalization (feeling or emotional). It is imperative to understand that we can only function within a single channel at any moment. In other words, one will work, but not two or all three at the same time. There is no such thing as multi-tasking. Most people on earth are visual creatures. For the general population the breakdown is:

Visual – 60%
Auditory – 30%
Internal – 10%

As you can see, the general population is 2 times more visual than the other Representational Channels. In earlier times, the 10% Internalization part of the population would be known as victims. This is my opinion as in earlier times, self-preservation was more difficult. If one spent too much time in self-dialogue or pity, they were consumed. The actual communication occurs by one or a combination of channels from these modalities as:

Verbally
Tonality – tone of voice
Non-verbally – body language

Keen sight has always been the primary channel for predators. Acute hearing has always been paramount for prey. This reflects back to our origins as a species. We have all heard of the "fight or flight" syndrome. What most probably has not heard of is the complete and more accurate name of "freeze, flight, fight, or fright" syndrome. These categories are correct in their function and order. There is a phase that occurs at the moment that our senses are heightened called a freeze. It is seen in the animal world by prey animals when they hear or sense something. They will freeze; their ears attentive and pupils expand as they try to determine the cause of the alert. In combat, the same thing occurs. When a soldier encounters an initial sign of threat, the response demanded by his military training and reinforced by other members of his unit, is the "stop, watch, and listen" heightened-alertness response. This is believed to have evolved from the prey trying to avoid detection because predators primarily detect moving objects rather than color.

The second most common reaction is the flight or fleeing from the source of the threat. Thirdly is the well-publicized response of fight. Lastly and even less thought about is a term known as fright. Fright is the body's defense mechanism of total surrender or playing dead. Many animals will play dead when excessively threatened in the wild. This can also play a bearing on why some females when victimized will simply surrender and allow whatever to take place to happen. Many in our society question why someone would just allow such an act to take place without resistance. It is the absolute surrender of yourself due to the threat. Generally, it is because the mind and body has surrendered to the amount of stress applied against it.

Police officers measured by their Representational Channels have been trained over time to change their percentages to best accommodate their function. Police Representational Channels on average are:

87% - Visual
7% - Auditory
6% - Internal

What this has created is an officer who is very astute to the visuals of the job. I am amazed with time and experience, how quickly and easily I could notice the small things that were a part of my job. I recognized the expired tag decal, the tampered temp tag, whether tint was illegal and guess almost dead on what the light transmittance was with a quick glance, the speed of approaching traffic, the driver wearing headsets, etc. They were small essentials of the job that I performed every day and became, like all officers, very efficient with the visuals. I remember once while searching the passenger's compartment of a car, opening a woman's purse on the front seat. I reached in and immediately found a bag with about an ounce of crack cocaine. This woman was standing behind me and to my left with my partner. As I reached into the bag, I saw her start to run in my peripheral vision. I instantly said aloud, "Nothing, there is nothing here." And I closed the purse and turned towards her and said, "Thanks for cooperating with us today." Nervously she replied, "Your welcome." I grabbed and handcuffed her. She yelled out, "But you said there was nothing there!" My peripheral vision, like that of a predator is attuned to movement.

We are better at noticing many things, yet still miss the most important. They are the simple movements and actions that in some way can be considered "micro expressions." These are not the simple fast twitch movements of the face that we associate with the meaning. I see it as a way to explain the simple things that occur which we commonly miss over the "large expression" items like, running the red light, speeding, observing a fight, or other law breaking violations. What I am discussing are simplistic things related to our survival. The behavior of a person(s) when they first noticed you such as: the way they walk is different with one arm having less movement, the blinker or brakes light of the car are left on after the stop, repetition of questions or statements, the heartbeat in their suprasternal notch, over talkative, dry mouth, wiping hands on their legs, etc. These are some of my noticeable micro expressions.

With this ramped up visual acumen comes other changes as well. One must always remember that we can only operate in a single channel at any one time. Our total abilities within the channels must always equal 100%. Therefore, by increasing our visual abilities, we must also decrease our other channels. As you can "see," our visuals increased to 87%, yet our auditory capacities decreased to a stunning 7% from the general populace percentile of 30. What does all of this mean? Police officers are some of the worse listeners. To improve these listening skills, we have to consciously and deliberately focus on our interviewing skills.

It is our job to conduct interviews with everyone we meet. During a traffic stop, a traffic crash, a domestic intervention, a pedestrian encounter, a burglary report, etc., we are conducting interviews. We conduct them constantly and fail to listen to what is being told to us. We over control the interviews because as police officers, we learn to control every situation to maintain an advantage. In interviewing, you have to learn the difference. Ask anyone outside of the profession and they will say that you are not a good listener. You have been programmed not to listen because of the above average visuals to see what others miss. In an interview though, it is our attention to listening details that will make us effective.

You are road side with a subject and questioning him and at the same time filling out a form, a ticket, complaint, or field interview. The inflection of their voice and response to your questions are critical. This is certainly a time that requires extra caution. You cannot write and listen at the same time with any proficiency. Again, one Representational Channel at a time. You can watch or listen, but not both. Otherwise, you will be asking questions, trying to listen to their response and write their answers down at the same time. While looking at them from several feet away, ask them the question and watch. Observe their behavior and response to the questions. If they provide a satisfactory answer, write the answer down when they are finished. If not, ask a clarifying question. Only write their response in the lull of time which occurs in between the questions. In other words; watch, listen, wait and then write.

Because of this transition of channels, new street officers who move to an investigators position will often find it difficult to interview with success. A determined effort is required to slow the process down and pay attention to the person. We also notice that the Internalization channel also reduces, but by only 4 percentage points from 10% to 6% of our totals. Emotional is not one of our strong points. Though sometimes visual, few on earth are more capable of repressing their feelings more than cops. The exception to this statement is in controlling an adrenaline rush from an incident that is almost overwhelming.

Written and recorded statements also fall within these rules. The words of a written statement express only 7% of the meaning that they intend. We can read a book and get a mental picture from the scene by a good writer and their use of punctuation. However, few of us have ever been moved by a written statement. The words can be easily misconstrued by each person's interpretation of the statement. A written statement can often mean a great deal to the prosecution team, yet mean little to members of the jury. A prosecutor will read the statement aloud with them. Why? It is to add the next means of effective communication to the words; tone of voice.

Tone of voice can change the meaning and the entire theme of the events. It adds an additional 38% of understanding to the words alone. Tone of voice, as we are learning, based on its consistency and use can place in other people's mind an idea whether you are an expert, shy, over-bearing, rude, polite, etc. When the jury reads, "That was when I yelled stop. Then I turned and ran down the street towards my cousin's house." The prosecutor will read it as "That was when I yelled, STOP! Then I turned and RAN, towards my cousin's house!" With the exclamation points and capitalization of the verbs to give them meaning, the sentence takes on more urgency. It is in this urgency that the prosecution tries to make you realize her desperation. As you read the sentences with the exclamation points, you are adding tone in your mind. This tone indicates the severity of the statement. The defense though will read it simply as it is written as if they had just finished playing and it was time to go home.

We now have the words themselves and the tone of voice, the equivalency of a tape recording. Together, we are receiving 45% of the information they are trying to express. What categories of expression are left to fill in the balance of 55%? There is only one, the visuals or body language that is associated with the words and tones. Our body language or rather the leaking of various clusters, creates the majority of information expressed. Watch a video of the same person who is making the statement and only then do you have the opportunity to grasp the meaning in its entirety.

To help us understand these thoughts, we need to explore our subconscious. It is in the subconscious that our ability to recognize things occurs. It is basically a built up collection of our experiences, the storage drive if you will. Our brains take in and process so much information; it is natural to conclude there is too much to accept. Nearly every day we experience an event that causes our mind to stop and wonder, "That looks familiar" or "That sounds familiar." As a police officer we often hear the phrase, "My hair on the back of my neck stood up." This may indicate that you have seen or heard something familiar to your sub conscious, but are unable to at once understand or recognize the trigger of this emotion. Body language is also recognized in the sub conscious. We will see things that cause us to react without hesitation. Our minds, because of the volume of information in the environment, will categorize everything into concepts and miss the details. It is the "I can see the forest, but not the trees" idea.

Where are we going with this and how does it apply to police work? It specifically affects one of the most dangerous occurrences in our profession, complacency. We recognize complacency as the cause of so many officer injuries and deaths. It happens with our subconscious and the training we provide for it. Let's say you average 10 traffic stops a day. Nothing of any significance occurs in 5 days of work. Therefore, you have made about 50 traffic stops where nothing has happened. Your subconscious relaxes and starts to relate these stops to no events. Your own subconscious is lowering your guards. These events are becoming "routine." On the 6th day, something happens which causes an adrenaline spike and you become cautious again. Yet over some time, it will slowly fade again.

To avoid this, place the importance and dangers of the stop in your mind manually. Think about the safety processes and pay attention to the events that are unfolding in front of you. Create a mental check list as we discussed earlier to use for the events you regularly encounter. This check list has to be followed to the "t" in order to prevent dangerous mistakes and stop the complacencies from happening.

There are many areas of behaviors which are critical to understand. We must evaluate each person as to the type of personality they have. For instance, are they introverts or extroverts? This will be demonstrated from their behaviors. How do they process information via the three representational channels of visual, auditory, or internal/emotional/Kinesthetic? Determine if they are optimist or pessimist, narcissistic or altruistic? Questions must appeal to the persons own individual programming or their predisposition toward one or the other at the time of the interview. Let's break these down.

The Representational Channels

1. Visuals – Most people will fall within this category because most of us are visually oriented. In fact 60% of the world's population is visually oriented. I have referred to this group as the primal predators. When speaking to these people they will have some of the following traits:
   - Eyes tend to move up
   - Head and posture is stiff and straight
   - Uses visual phrases (see chart below)
     o Let's <u>look</u> at it differently.
     o <u>See</u> how this works for you.
     o I can't quite <u>picture</u> it.
     o Let's draw a <u>diagram</u> or <u>map</u>.
     o I never forget a <u>face</u>.
   - They speak and breathe rapidly
   - Have an unrestrained voice tone
   - Rapid movements
2. Auditory – These are people who gather most of their information from sound. They are the students who can tape record a class lecture and comprehend the most by listening to the recording later. I refer to this group as the prey. Only 30% of the population is within this category. These people will have the following traits:
   - Eyes tend to go to the sides
   - A slight head tilt
   - A relaxed posture
   - Some gestures and movements
   - Uses auditory phrases like
     o Clear as a bell.
     o Earful
     o Hold your tongue.

- To tell the truth
- Voiced an opinion.
- Speaks and breathes at a moderate pace

3. Internal/Emotional/Kinesthetic – This involves only 10% of the population. These individuals are what I call "the victims." Always remember that these percentages can change for every individual at any given time based on the circumstances. We all possess some of each of these traits and they expose themselves accordingly in relation to the events we experience. You could be a highly visual subject but when faced with the death of a loved one, switch emotions internally. It is the baseline for each subject under normal circumstances which we are determining. These people will have the following traits:
   - Speaks and moves slowly with a low tone
   - Eyes tend to go down
   - Slumped posture
   - Few if any gestures
   - Slow controlled breathing
   - Uses Kinesthetic phrases
     - All washed up
     - Get in control
     - Hang in there
     - Hold it or hold on
     - Stiff upper lip

NEUROLINGUISTIC EXERCISES

The human brain is divided into two hemispheres; one side is used for storing factual information while the other side is used for creating new information. If you focus closely on an individual's eye movement during the fact gathering portion of the interview, you will be able to determine which hemisphere the person is referencing when gathering factual information and/or creating new information and potentially lying.

If you ask a person a question which they may not expect, it requires them to seek the answer in their stored memory. If the question is not threatening to them, they will look high and to their left to recall the answer if they are right handed. I refer to this as seeking the correct "file in a cabinet" to retrieve. If you ask repetitive questions within the same area, they may not react the same. The file was opened and the information retrieved. There will not be a necessity to seek the information because the "file" was opened at the first question and the brain has reviewed the contents. A better approach is to ask a question followed by another after they answer, but on a different topic. After questioning them through a series of issues, you can now return to the original subject. The file on that information has slowly begun to close as they were required to open other areas in the "cabinet." Their reaction will be more pronounced and you will be able to observe their response for comparison to the earlier answers.

Below are the question categories that apply to the different Representational Channels. These are standardized for a right handed person. Each person interviewed must be evaluated to determine their own baseline.

Visual Recall
- What is your social security number?
- What side of the front door is the door knob on?
- What is the seventh letter of the alphabet?
- What did you wear this past Saturday?

- How many windows are in your house?
- What is the first thing you see when you open your front door?
- What was the color of your first bicycle?
- List all of the different colors in your bedroom.

Visual Constructed
- Describe your dream date.
- Imagine yourself as a four foot person playing basketball against the Lakers
- Imagine yourself completely bald wearing a tuxedo.

Auditory Recall
- What are the last six words in the Pledge of Allegiance?
- What was the last song you heard on the radio?
- What sound of nature do you like best?
- What is the fifth word in the national anthem?
- What is the chorus in your favorite song?

Auditory Construct
- If you could ask the President any two questions, what would they be?
- Describe the sound of a vehicle horn becoming a flute and then a drumroll.
- Describe the way you would sound if you tried to talk under water.
- Describe the basic sounds of the Chinese language as you have heard it.

Kinesthetic
- Imagine the feeling of ice cream melting in your hand.
- Describe in detail how you felt this morning immediately after getting out of bed.
- How did you feel the first time you experienced a plane ride?

- If you have ever been sea sick, describe how it came on you and how you felt throughout.

A quick guide to recognizing these automatic, unconscious eye movements, or "eye accessing cues," that often accompany particular thought processes are:

- Eyes Up and Left: Non-dominant hemisphere visualization - i.e., remembered imagery.
- Eyes Up and Right: Dominant hemisphere visualization - i.e., constructed imagery and visual fantasy.
- Eyes Lateral Left: Non-dominant hemisphere auditory processing - i.e., remembered sounds, words, and "tape loops" and tonal discrimination.
- Eyes Lateral Right: Dominant hemisphere auditory processing - i.e., constructed sounds and words
- Eyes Down and Left: Internal dialogue, or inner self-talk.
- Eyes Down and Right: Feelings, both tactile and visceral.
- Eyes Straight Ahead, but Defocused or Dilated: Quick access of almost any sensory information; but usually visual.

PERSONALITY

Next we want to determine if they are an optimist or pessimist, narcissistic or altruistic. This will be established by our initial questioning. It helps to understand what a person's normal mental state is to determine a baseline. We will determine what their standard is so any changes are recognizable. This would include a pessimistic person suddenly becoming an optimist or vice versa. These types of changes indicate an occurrence which is altering their baseline and may indicate deception. Some sample questioning during an interview would be:

Sample Questions	Optimist vs. Pessimist
How are you today?	Good vs. Not bad
How's the diet?	I'm keeping the weight off vs. I'm not gaining
Still having trouble at work?	I'm still there vs. I haven't quit
How's that car in rain?	It holds the road vs. It doesn't slip
Why did you buy that car?	Good price vs. It wasn't expensive
Why did you move there?	Nice neighborhood vs. Not a lot of crime

Some sample statements once it appears they may confess would be:

Sample Statements	Optimist vs. Pessimist

You will sleep better if you confess vs. No more sleepless nights if you confess
You will have a clear conscious vs. You won't feel so guilty all the time
You'll feel better if you get this off your chest vs. You'll stop feeling stressed
You need to take responsibility vs. You need to stop lying
You need to come forward with the truth vs. You need to stop hiding the truth

Sample Statements	Narcissist vs. Altruist

Look yourself in the mirror vs. Look your wife in the eye (children in the face)
Doing what's best for you vs. Doing what's best for your family
Be the type of person you want to be vs. Be the type of person your parents raised
Take responsibility because you vs. Take responsibility because you know it's the right thing to do
You want to do what's right vs. You want people to know that you did what's right

You want to be honest vs. You want people to know you're an honest person

They can be emotional or reality based personalities in addition to being an introvert or extrovert. All of these areas have to be examined and close attention paid to their behaviors and verbal responses. An emotional based person will react to things in an emotional manner. An introvert may also display behaviors that are perceived as deception when in fact it is their normal display. This will be an important topic later in the book regarding false confessions or interviewing bias. Therefore, they are best dealt with in a sympathetic approach. Look and listen for signals such as:

- Shame
- Embarrassment
- Remorse
- Shyness
- Genuine concern over their problem
- Obviously controlled
- Nervous or worried
- Artistic or sees life as a fairy tail
- Verbalizes frustration, despair, and negative emotions
- Inconsistent behavior

A reality based personality can be seen as someone who thinks, organizes and plans activities on a logical scale. They are best dealt with on a rational or logical approach. Look and listen for signals such as:

- Lack of genuine emotion
- Lack of remorse
- No shame over the events
- Thinks and talks in facts and figures
- Analyzes
- Thinks in a step by step fashion
- Consistent behavior

- Very aware of all consequences

An introvert personality will show signs of one who prefers to internalize stress. They comprise only 25% of the population.
- They do not make friends easily yet they may have 1 or 2 close friends.

The extrovert personality is the majority of people making up 75% of the populace. They will be:

- Are energized to be around other people
- Fade or get bored when they are left alone
- Is susceptible to confusion
- Doesn't mind their body space being infringed
- Concerned what others may think about them
- Forms quick attachments
- Less likely to show nerves and inhibitions
- Likes bright and flashy clothes
- Loves excitement
- Readily responds to questioning
- Less controlled emotional state

Once you have recognized the person as reality or emotion plus introvert or extrovert, you can exploit the information in an interview.

For an Emotion Based Introvert you can:
- Display total belief in their guilt
- Review the evidence every few minutes
- Compliment them on some personal trait
- Dominate with eye contact and touch
- Rationalize and project constantly
- Be subdued and private
- Point out their mental symptoms of guilt
- Use family, friends and associates against them
- Minimize constantly
- Express your own friendship towards them

- Show empathy to their problems
- Touch them reassuringly
- Wear natural colors

For an Emotion Based Extrovert you can:
- Try to confuse them
- Point to the futility of denying
- Dress should convey status of authority (best suit)
- Appeal constantly to their pride (flatter or challenge pride)
- Be slow and deliberate, emphasize key words and phrases, use lots of silence at key moments
- Use family, friends, and associates against the subject (those who are important)
- For some males who are not strongly extroverted, touching can establish dominance
- The interrogation format should not be tightly controlled

For a Reality Based Introvert you can:
- Gain dominance early
- Dress in natural colors
- Approach should be well organized
- Be subdued and private
- Evaluate carefully before touching this person
- Use props (have photos, evidence, etc. handy)
- Use a matter of fact approach
- Cover facts chronologically or systematically
- Emphasize physical and testimonial evidence
- Approach them with no warmth, be straight forward (niceness is viewed as a weakness by them)

For a Reality Based Extrovert you can:
- point out futility in denying
- Use a matter of fact approach
- Dress forcefully
- Be patient and persistent

- Use questions with "yes" or "no" answer
- Speak slightly louder than normal
- Appeal constantly to their pride (flatter or challenge pride)
- Use a well-organized approach, be chronological or otherwise systematic with case facts
- Approach them with no warmth, be straight forward (niceness is viewed as a weakness by them)
- Have as much evidence as possible readily available (props/bluffs/photo's/charts/anything plausible)
- Interrogation format should not be tightly controlled
- Strictly adhere to one on one interview/interrogation format From the beginning, try to pull the subject into the conversation
- Never show doubt or pause when speaking, be optimistic about the subjects guilt
- Subject will drift if not controlled, keep to the matter at hand
- Once he/she has opened up, be practical and concrete at all times
- If nothing else works, use realistic language

The Interviews

9

Good detection spares us from unwelcome surprises.

- Barton Whaley

There are numerous areas of an interview that requires examination. This is a complex process that can take years to learn. There have been many studies conducted on what it takes to be a good interviewer. Sadly, people today gather their ideas of reality from television and the internet. Just as a movie may announce, it is "based on a true story," even if the story was about you, after watching what had been created we would not recognize the events. This is how most of the ideas surrounding an interview are perceived. Yes, anyone can sit down and ask questions of someone else and receive an answer. In the world of law enforcement, the business world, and even the military, much more has to be obtained. The stakes can be as high as life threatening to job loss.

There are skills which can be learned that separate an average from a superior interviewer. In fact, The Department of Defense, Defense Academy for Credibility Assessment group known as DACA conducted a two year study called: Final Report, May 2007, MIPR#H9C101-G-0051, Assessment of Optimal Interrogation Approaches. The study discovered 17 areas that differentiate superior interrogators from others. These areas are:

1. Preparations for the Interview
2. Develops Themes
3. Builds Rapport
4. Rationalizes and Minimalizes the criminal act
5. Uses Optional Questions
6. Confronts the Subjects
7. Recognizes non-verbal cues
8. Treats the Suspect with respect
9. Shows a Professional Image
10. Separates self from police/authorities
11. Reinforces/rewards/thanks admissions and acts
12. Controls own emotion
13. Maintains a matter of fact approach to questioning
14. Does not allow backtracking
15. Uses hope and fear
16. Allows the suspect to explain what happened in their own words
17. Uses recapping – after confession, has suspect repeat from beginning to end

When conducting an interview, to reasonably evaluate the meaning of the statement made, we must understand the various levels of communication. Special attention must be given to the verbal, non-verbal, tone, and proxemics of the individual. With these issues in mind, when a person is telling the truth, the verbal, non-verbal, and tone will complement each other to create the total message. Merely evaluating the spoken word as most people will can only be effective if the person being interviewed is truthful throughout the interview. When a person is being deceitful, the verbal, non-verbal, tone etc. will contradict each other. If the subject is trying to deceive you, evaluating only the spoken word will miss much of the message and have limited success.

For most people the interview is more like an interrogation. Because of our police trained, dominate attitude, we tend to do the following:

- We allow our police minds to dominate the entire process.
- We talk as much if not more than they do.
- We tend to keep everything non personal with a "just the facts" attitude.
- We pass by the rapport phase and tend to not pay attention because we already know where we want this to go.

In fact, especially in the beginning of the interview, we need rapport. If I could replace the word interrogation with the words "investigative interview," it could help us relax more and have a better connection to the interview. This is when we need, in addition to rapport, to determine a baseline of their behaviors, detect deceptions, and evaluate themes.

Time has to be taken for this progression to succeed. If you start to take short cuts, you are defeating the entire reasons to initiate the interview. Our position in the beginning is to allow them to do the talking. As police officers, we like to be in control. With two ears and one mouth, we should listen twice as much as we talk. Ask the questions to keep the interview moving. Do not do anything except listen and observe. Remember, there is no such thing as actual multi-tasking. Watch and listen, do not write.

The process begins the moment you enter the room with the subject. Never forget that everything can rest upon the first impression you make. Now is the time to take away your police persona and replace it with that of a "friend." They will not always realize it, but from the time you enter the room they are evaluating you. They will determine "friend or foe" almost instantly.

Proxemics

The distance required from another person to feel comfortable based on the circumstances.
- Intimate- touching to 1.5 feet
- Personal/Business – 1.5 – 4 feet

- Social – 4 – 7 feet
- Public – out as far as 12-25 feet

A little known fact, but on a different scale, is that lion trainers use proxemics to their advantage. Though the whip and gun is exciting and demonstrates falsely their control, distance is maintained with proxemics. The large cats have a natural instinct to back away from someone until they can no more. The trainer will move towards the cats which naturally cause them to move away against the cage wall. Once they cannot move any further they begin to advance on the trainer always in a straight line. The trainer will monitor their movement and place a stool between them and immediately back away. The cat will leap onto the stool, but will not advance because the trainer has moved back out of their space.

It has been found that people will perform a set of actions whenever their personal space is intruded upon without permission. First they will start to rock, leg swing or tap. This shows that tension is building. Then they will close their eyes, lower their chin and hunch their shoulders. Finally, when nothing else has worked, they will get up and leave. The psychological pressure placed on someone is immense.

In our police academies, stress is added to determine which recruits have the fortitude to withstand the strain. Police work carries with it a tremendous amount of stress. Some people are better adapted to cope with the stress than others. The military and law enforcement tries to fill their ranks with those personnel capable of withstanding more than most. There will come a day in their lives that the level of stress will exceed anything most people will ever endure. Our goal is to survive this moment with a clear thinking mind. The best example and one of the most recognizable is a drill instructor giving commands.

RAPPORT

Rapport is the condition of mutual trust and understanding between the interviewer and interviewee. Many witnesses and suspects feel uneasy about providing accusatory information. Resistance to the disclosure of information is increased if the interviewer is a total stranger.

There are techniques necessary for building rapport. Most people have never given this topic consideration and assume they simply walk in and say "Hi" and that is rapport building. There are techniques that can be utilized and are universal in acceptance, but they will not work on each person. Therefore, it is critical for you understand some rules to building rapport.

- Begin by commenting on a topic of interest to the suspect. Your prior collection of background information should help to provide this information.
- Establish confidence and friendliness by engaging in topics about current events such as: weather; news; TV shows and sports.
- Display pleasant emotional responses and avoid distasteful expressions.

- Don't ask questions in the beginning that lead the suspect to believe that you are suspicious of them.
- Appear interested and sympathetic to his concerns.
- Going through the biographical data will help establish rapport. It also alerts you to information that could be used in the interrogation.
- Don't begin an interrogation until you feel that some form of rapport has been established.

Avoid these areas when attempting to establish rapport:

- Don't sneer or ridicule the suspect.
- Don't bully or try to impress the suspect with your importance.
- Don't make any deliberate false promises.
- Don't belittle the suspect or his position.
- Try not to reveal signs of your own personal beliefs because they may be in contradiction with the suspect's.
- Don't yell, curse or try to alienate the person.

LISTENING

In order to be a successful interviewer, one has to do the single thing that cops do the least; listen. Police officers are some of the worse listeners because we are taught from our entry into the academy to take charge. We have to watch for everything big or small which has increased the visual Representational Channel above the general populace percentages. They changed from 60% visual to 87%, 30% auditory to 7%, and 10% Kinesthetic to 6%. The profession has changed the ways police officers are able to receive the information from those who are trying to communicate. It is pounded into us from day one to watch. However, as one changes so must the others to maintain 100%. Therefore, auditory and kinesthetic have fallen even further, auditory the most. There are several methods we can use for listening; I refer to them as interested continuators. They demonstrate that you are listening to keep the conversation moving forward.

A study from the University of Missouri indicates that many of us spend 70 to 80 percent of our waking hours in some form of communication. Of that time, we spend about 9 percent writing, 16 percent reading, 30 percent speaking, and 45 percent listening. Ironically, we already know that most of us are poor listeners. There are several reasons according to the study.

Even though listening is the communication skill we use the most, it is also the skill in which we've had the least training. We've had much more formal training in other communication skills — writing, reading, and speaking. In fact, very few persons have had any extended formal training in listening.

Another reason for poor listening skills is that we can think faster than someone else can speak. Most of us speak at the rate of about 125 words per minute. However, we have the mental capacity to understand someone speaking at 400 - 500 words per minute. This difference means that when we listen to the average speaker, we're using only 25 percent of our mental capacity. We still have 75 percent to do something else with, so our minds wander. A concentrated effort is needed to stay focus before our minds begin to tune into other ideas.

Passive Listening – Never express any of your own ideas or judgments. Instead, invite the person to share their feelings and thoughts. Stay with simple verbal responses like:

> "Really"
> "I see"
> "How about that"
> "No kidding"

Non-verbal responses like:
> Nodding
> Smiling/frowning
> Raising your eyebrows

More direct responses are:
> "I'd like to hear more about that"
> "Tell me the whole story"
> "This seems pretty important to you"

Active Listening - This type of listening is much more effective than passive listening and will assist in building rapport and establishing normative behavior. It identifies what the person is feeling and/or what the message really means. Every message contains two parts:
- The content or factual material
- The speaker's feelings or attitude toward the content

You can put the message into your own words and see if that was what the subject meant. Never be judgmental or act like your giving advice.

There are three areas of active listening:
- Paraphrase (rephrasing): repeat mentally and/or out loud to the subject what has been said.
- Clarifying: ask the speaker to repeat, clarify, or simplify
- Summarizing: after the speaker has provided information on one subject, review the information with the speaker

When active listening always:
- make good eye contact
- be patient
- pay close attention
- keep on subject until the thought is complete

Never:
- interrupt
- rush the person

- finish the person's sentence/thought
- look at watch or have wandering eyes
- fidget with pen or pencil
- write things down
- never send back a message of advice or judgment
- never include your opinion unless its expressly asked for or you know it will match the subjects

Robert Montgomery conducted workshops using business executives to learn what they considered effective listening. He surveyed the participating executives on the characteristics of the worst listeners they know. The usual replies are:

- Always interrupts.
- Jumps to conclusions.
- Finishes my sentences.
- Is inattentive; has wandering eyes and poor posture.
- Changes the subject.
- Writes down everything.
- Doesn't give any response.
- Is impatient.
- Loses temper.
- Fidgets with a pen or pencil nervously.

Characteristics of good listeners -
- Looks at me while I'm speaking.
- Questions me to clarify what I'm saying.
- Shows concerns by asking me about my feelings.
- Repeats some of the things I say.
- Doesn't rush me.
- Is poised and emotionally controlled.
- Reacts responsively with a nod of the head, a smile, or a frown.
- Pays close attention.
- Doesn't interrupt me.
- Keeps on the subject till I've finished my thoughts.

In studies which involve listening, several areas are essential to becoming a good listener. It is considered helping the speaker and can be summed up as the golden rule of listening: a listener should listen to others as they would like to be listened to themselves. In a criminal investigative interview, you have to appear genuinely interested in what the suspect is saying. This helps to facilitate more information. To accomplish this, everything relies on the listener's outward behaviors and is entirely visual. To help the subject or speaker perform successfully, a listener needs to do four things:

- Avoid distracting verbal comments - This includes not interrupting, changing the subject, finishing sentences for the speaker, or interjecting with "yes, uh-huh" as though on autopilot.
- Avoid distracting nonverbal actions - This includes not fidgeting, slumping, staring blankly, or smiling and nodding in agreement as though on autopilot.
- Offer verbal encouragement and support - This includes everything from a genuine, "Yes, I see," to rescuing a speaker who has been interrupted or lost his or her train of thought with cues like, "You were just saying . . ." or "I think you also wanted to say something about . . . ."
- Offer nonverbal encouragement and support - This includes looking alert and plugged into the conversation by sitting up straight, maintaining eye contact, and responding with facial expressions that are appropriate for the speaker's message.

Distracting behaviors, whether verbal or nonverbal, are to be avoided for two reasons. First, because they may be considered disrespectful towards the speaker, distracting behaviors may prevent the speaker from sharing their ideas. Secondly, they create a loss in the listener's concentration. Encouraging behaviors help prove to the speaker that the listener is paying attention and they reinforce the listener's efforts to keep paying attention. That is, a listener is more likely to stay mentally tuned in when they are leaning forward and maintaining eye contact with the speaker than when he or she is writing on a note pad or looking out the window.

DECEPTION

Deception is a social norm. It has been concluded in many studies that an individual's success can be enhanced in any task when a certain amount of deceit is implemented at some point. Additionally, it is believed that individuals who are well versed in deception tend to be more successful than those who are not. As a result of this social requirement for deception, all humans lie. Human nature is a daily exercise in deceit, yet lying does not come naturally nor is it easy. When a person lies, they undergo a physiological change in an effort to make a lie believable. The untruthful person's physiology:

- The liar will feel threatened by the questions which are part of the specific issue
- If the liar does not convince you of his truthfulness, they are aware of the potential consequences
- Being aware of the consequences is what triggers the fight, flight or freeze response
- In an attempt to mask and contain physiological responses, verbal and non-verbal indicators of deception leak out.

When we perform a conscious action which changes reality in some way, the following factors apply:

1. The action is not automatic, it's produced
2. The person's cognitive thinking processes involve some degree of rehearsal and consideration of the

probable results of the action before it's carried out. Impulsive actions are exception to this process.

3. What may seem to be an impulsive act may have been imagined or fantasized countless times over the person's lifespan. An example would be a pedophile.

4. A combination of incidents may serve as a catalyst in causing one's impulsive behavior

5. Many criminals think about, plan, scheme and mentally rehearse their crimes prior to putting them into action

For the following signs of a truthful or deceitful person, remember that any single issue may not be indicative of the category. We are always looking at clusters of behavior. A falsehood will result if someone says, "He crossed his leg during the interview therefore he must be lying." This singular act is in the deceitful column but by itself means nothing. It shall be observed and remembered in the event other actions take place.

Signs of a Truthful Person:
- Appears at ease
- Talkative
- Sincere
- Cooperative
- Answers questions directly
- Maintains good eye contact
- Generally appears relaxed
- Lighthearted conversation

Signs of a Deceptive Person:
- Apprehensive
- Worried appearance
- Much sighing or yawning
- Excessive movement
- Dreamy air
- Overly friendly
- Poor eye contact
- Evasive answering

- Aggressive toward the interviewer

Sitting postures can reveal a lot about a person. A Truthful Person will:
- Sits upright
- Relaxed looking
- Faces interviewer
- Does not lean away
- Changes positions smoothly
- Arms open & uncrossed
- Legs open & uncrossed
- Head & shoulders aligned
- Overall appearance casual

A Deceptive Person Will:
- Slouches or sits stiff and rigid
- Shies away from interviewer
- Arms close to side and crossed
- Moves frequently and rapidly
- Faces to the side/leans toward the door
- Head slumped

Facial Expressions

No single facial expression is indicative of guilt or deception. The head, because it is closest to the brain and we are most aware of it, is easiest to control. An example of this is a calm facial expression with a lot of arm and leg movement which indicates high stress.

Facial color changes: Flushing is a good sign that stress is present. Facial color changes usually conform to the following pattern:

- Face becomes white or turns pale = height of "fight or flight"
- Face turns red or reddish = recovery from strong emotion

- Skin turns dark = blood backing up due to constricted veins

Muscle spasms take the form of facial grimaces or muscle constrictions in various parts of the body, especially on the head. These uncontrollable muscle movements will sometimes include the arms and legs, and in a high percentage of the cases, are good indicators of deception. The cheeks or the area around the eyes tremble uncontrollably which is indicative of stress. This is a reaction I have observed countless of times in my career when interviewing someone. To see it, you have to pay close attention.

The eyes (excluding neurolinguistics):
   a. The most expressive part of the head is the eyes
   b. The following eye movement may indicate a problem
      1. Excessive eye shifting
      2. Prolonged eye contact
      3. Staring at the interviewer
      4. Abnormal eye contact
   c. It is possible for eye contact to be too good. This is usually an aggressive stare down which is an attempt to dominate you and/or is the result of the false belief that a truthful person will always look you in the eye.
   d. Any break in eye contact, which is timely and not part of the norm, is a sign of stress
   f. Breaks in eye contact can be disguised in a number of ways:
      1. Placing your hand to rub your forehead or other facial area is a form of a break in eye contact
      2. Blinking will increase when a person is under stress

The nose:
- Touching or rubbing the nose indicates stress and/or deception
- Holding the nose between the finger and thumb means "that stinks" or "that smells"
- Sometimes a nose touch is combined with other signs to yield a single movement cluster

The mouth:
- A big smile on the mouth of the subject is not realistic
- Phony smiles are generally upper teeth smiles
- Any obstruction of speech indicates stress and/or deception
- Biting lips
- Squeezing lips together
- Continually licking lips and they remain dry
- Dry mouth making clicking noises
- Strings of thick saliva between teeth and/or lips
- White foam at the corners of the mouth

The hands:
- A change in the activity of the hands
- Grooming, lint picking
- Scratching, rubbing, massaging
- Flipping the hands away indicates the desire to throw away unpleasant subject
- A hand to the throat shows stress, indicates sore spot
- Playing with fingernails
- Drumming fingers, as the tension increases, drumming becomes faster and louder

Crossing of any parts of the body may indicate defensiveness, protectiveness, etc. This emotion can be caused by general fear of the situation or by guilt induced stresses which may reduce the information intake of the subject.

Meanings of crossed arms:
- Arms crossed tightly in front of chest with fists = uncooperative, cocky
- Arms crossed closely to neck = high level of resistance
- Arms crossed while leaning toward interviewer = very defensive, uncooperative
- A crossing can be, and often is, combined with other gestures

Legs and Feet
- Crossing of the legs has the same general meaning as the crossing of the arms
- Figure 4 leg cross indicates cockiness
- Feet or legs in a V shape indicates confidence
- Putting feet up on chair or desk, moving your chair with their feet, or dragging their chair away from you is an attempt to dominate
- At moments of stress, the legs may:
  1. Cross for the first time
  2. Un-cross for the first time
  3. Change direction of crossing
  4. Legs crossed, upper foot bounces gently (rise in blood pressure)
  5. Legs crossed, upper legs shows fast, forceful swing (impatience or anger)
- Knees wobbling back and forth is a sign of great tension
- Other leg movement indicative of deception:
  1. One leg stretched out in front of the other
  2. Both knees up under chin with feet on chair (rare, generally in females)
  3. Hand placed on inside of leg, trying to comfort self
  4. Toes turn up to point back at self
  5. Feet going under chair/ coming out from under the chair
  6. Ankles crossed under chair

7. Feet twitching
8. Toes rising, feet rolling
9. Tapping feet is indicative of agitation

Religious behaviors:
- Praying
- Holding religious items
- Singing gospels
- Raising hands to take oath, "scouts honor"
- Invoking a deity or swearing to God
- Swearing on the souls or life of a loved one

Expressions

10

The wish to relieve guilt may motivate a confession, but the wish to avoid the humiliation of shame may prevent it.

-   Paul Ekman

There are many people in the world that can be considered an expert on expressions. Typically, we like to think of micro-expressions which were made popular by television shows like "Lie to Me." In reality, the professional consultant for the show, Paul Ekman, is one of the world's foremost authorities on the subject.

I will, for this examination of the topics include all of the physical expressions made by people in all areas of the body. It is imperative to understand a few simple rules about reading expressions. Some people who are pathological recognize that others are looking for certain behaviors and they will make efforts to compensate. For instance, we all know that one of the key factors is eye contact. It has been shown that most people have a hard time maintaining eye contact when they are telling a lie. However, some people know this and maintain a strong eye contact.

Everyone should expect pacifying behaviors from persons being interviewed. The limbic system plays a key role. When someone gets nervous, the stressor will begin to create energy which has to be used. This excess of energy will be displayed as pacifying behaviors. Pacifying behaviors are selective to each individual. Some may twirl their hair, press their lips, rub their neck or thighs, and even their fingers, nose, or bridge of their nose. This can be normal especially at the beginning of an interview as nervousness is natural. The activities should begin to reduce as you build rapport. Watch for an increase in behavior frequency and chatter. If the subject is chewing gum, ask them to spit it out so they are not aided in stress release.

When asking questions, be sure to take your time. Ask the question and wait to watch their reactions. Stress that increases and decreases will often be displayed by how they sit and their pacifying behaviors. An example of this is when they lean back, if they put their feet under the chair they are trying to create distance.

Behavior clues have to be examined in clusters. Just because someone does one thing that we have talked about does not mean they are lying. In fact most of what we have discussed simply demonstrates that a person is nervous. It becomes your job to determine the reasoning behind the nerves. As was said before, you must ask the questions and observe the behaviors which need to appear in clusters or groups. Observe the person as they sit in their chair in the open, not against anything that will give them support. Let's examine the human body:

Feet and legs – They are the furthest from the brain. We first have to look for their normal behavior and then watch for change.

- If they constantly bounce their legs or feet and then suddenly stop or if they sit still and then bounce, ask yourself why?
- If they suddenly turn their toes inward or interlock their feet, they are insecure or feel threatened.
- Foot kicking is a subconscious act of resisting something unpleasant.
- If they have their legs crossed and are jiggling their foot and then start kicking the foot, they are not happy.

- Their feet lock behind the chair legs and they rub their thighs – very stressed
- They move their foot from in front to under the chair is a sign of distancing.
- Happy feet, feet/legs that bounce with joy, are the result of a positive emotion.
- We tend to turn toward things we like and turn away from things that we don't like.
- If a person who is sitting down clasps both hands on his knees then this is a sign he wants to leave.
- Gravity defying behaviors of the feet (pointing a foot upward off the ground, heel to the ground) are positive cues. People with depression rarely exhibit gravity defying behaviors.
- Leg splays, a dominant stance, often communicates that something is wrong.
- Recognizing our leg-splay posture during a heated exchange and adjusting will often lessen the confrontation level and reduce the tension.
- Leg crossing is a display of comfort. If you're standing with your legs crossed you are comfortable with your surroundings (you're not in a "get away fast" position) or with the person you're speaking with. Also, when you cross your legs in company you may subconsciously tilt toward the person you favor most.
- A woman will often play with her shoes and dangle them from her toes when she is comfortable with her companion
- Seated leg crosses when people sit side by side, the direction of their leg crosses become significant. If they are on good terms, the top leg crossed over will point toward the other person.

Torso – This is not a commonly thought of body portion and it is not as recognizable to the person who is affected by it either.

- Trying to lean back or distancing

- Turn slightly away shows a dislike
- Lean into or towards someone or something that interest us
- Crossing our arm or placing something between you at the torso is shielding
- Can be not as noticeable but has the same effect as arm crossing is the playing with a tie, shirt or cufflinks etc.
- Splaying in a chair, sitting with legs spread over chair and facing the back is disrespectful or the dominating of the area
- If you move into their personal space, they sit more straight is a sign of respect or concern
- Chest puffing or jacket removal – fight preparation
- Half shoulder shrugs – they are not committed to their answer
- Slow or weak shoulder rise – lack confidence or uncomfortable
- Full strong shoulder shrug shows confidence

Arms – follows the rules of gravity.

- When they defy gravity like raising of the arms – joy or excitement
- Weight of gravity drags the shoulders down as well – depressed or upset
- Arms at sides or across chest – worried or protective
- Arms behind back – at your mercy or consider myself above you, court or regal stance
- Elbows away from body shows to keep your distance or shows authority while against your waist shows weakness
- Hooding – placing and interlocking fingers behind your head creating a cobra like hood is a show of dominance. Supervisors will often do this at meetings. A sign of dominance.

Think about all of the arm movements that exist in a relationship and their subconscious meanings. Hugs, holding hands, jewelry and tattoos, handshakes, nail biting, hand wringing, steepling (confidence), thumbs up or down and the list continues.

Face – there are so many facets of the face, the eyes, mouth, nose, blushing, tremors, etc.

- Small pupils - do not like what we see
- Large pupils – we like what we see or we see danger
- High eyebrows – confidence
- Low eyebrows – dislike
- Eye blocking – squinting shows concern or dislike
- Closing eyes – block out negatives
- Gaze away during conversation – comfort display or clarity of thought, not rude
- Roving eyes – disinterested or superior
- Rapid eye blinks – inner struggle or stress
- Looking askance – sideways glance or untrusting
- Lip pursing – person rejects what is said
- Thin lips – stress
- Sneer – act of contempt
- Licking the lips – stressed
- Biting the lips – insecure
- Furrowed forehead – frowning – sad
- Nose flare – aroused or intent to do something physical
- Blushing – deep emotional states
- Blanching (turning pale) – shock or high stress
- Crinkle nose – dislike
- Chin down – lacks confidence

A quote from Dr. Birdwhistell, former professor of research in anthropology at Temple University (who initiated basic work in the science of kinesics) warned that "no body position or movement, in and of itself, has a precise meaning." In other words, we cannot always say that crossed arms mean, 'I will not let you in,' or that rubbing the nose with a finger means disapproval or rejection, and steepling the fingers superiority. These are naive interpretations of kinesics. Sometimes they are only true in the context of the entire behavior pattern of a person. Body language and spoken language, Dr. Birdwhistell believes, are dependent on each other. Spoken language alone will not give us the full meaning of what a person is saying, nor can body language alone give us the full meaning. If we listen only to the words when someone is talking, we may get as much of a distortion as we would if we listened only to the body language.

Even though we have looked at many possible meanings for various behaviors, they have to be taken into context with what is said and asked based upon their identified baseline. Take posture as an example. There are many things we can examine that we do every day that are directly linked to posture. There is only so much time that you can observe a person's behavior without making them aware of it as well as being able to consciously focus on everything that is occurring. Most people will have head movements during a conversation. There is usually a specific head movement at the end of a statement which serves as a signal to the other person to start his answer. This activity, not consciously recognized, serves to expedite a conversation so we are not required to say we are finished, your turn.

Often times a rise in voice pitch at the end of a word indicates a question has been asked. This is usually added with a raise in the head position. Ask yourself a question and notice these subtle occurrences. "What time is it?" or "Where are you going?" Other body parts will rise like the eyelids or even your hands or arms. When we are making a statement, the voice tone and head movement will lower at the end of the last word. These are referred to as linguistic markers. They are the physical aids to the language. If the speaker intends to continue his statement, they will not change their voice pitch, head movement, eyes or hands as a "marker" to you that they are not yet finished.

Writers and movie makers have a keen understanding of how these head movements play into our appearance. If they intend to characterize a "cool" or stoic person, one who does not flinch under pressure nor has no emotional attachment, they teach them to talk without head or face movements. Most people will move their heads at least every couple of sentences as well as side glances, stance adjustments, blinks, touches etc. To contrast this, think of a runway model. They are taught to be emotionless and stoic as they move down the aisle. They hold themselves rigid and unnatural to force everyone to subconsciously recognize the mannequin like exposure.

Body positions are another example. When in a social setting, most persons shift through two to four positions. Rarely does one position last more than twenty minutes. When under stress, people have a tendency to adjust more often. Think about someone listening to a speaker in a specific position of leaning back in their chair. When the speaker reaches a point that the listener disagrees with, they change their position. They lean forward into a position of rebuttal. When he is finished, they generally return to the original position. Again I stress that a change in posture signifies that something has happened, not what has happened.

Masking emotions is a common process that everyone uses to conceal their true feelings. By masking I mean even though you are mad, you smile. The most common way to mask emotions is with a smile. It is one of our first learned expressions to show happiness or to get a positive response from another.

A husband catches his wife talking low and it sounds like she is talking to another man, he may confront her. She of course denies the affair, but her overall body language in conjunction with word usage will betray her. If you bump into someone accidentally, it is common to smile as a sign of apology. Masking is something we do all day long. It also accounts for many of our behaviors when we are not in public. All day long we are forced to smile and be courteous even though most of the time we would have preferred to get angry with someone. This built up behavior resistance that occurs all day is released when we are not in public. In the drive home, you yell and cuss the other drivers. Your behavior at home takes a while to calm and your significant other has learned over time to leave you alone and knows you will get over it all.

Lie Detection from Emotion

The stronger the emotion involved in a lie and the greater the number of different emotions, the more likely it is the lie will be betrayed by behavioral leakage. According to Dr. Paul Ekman, guilt is an emotion more problematic for the liar. It causes leakage and the torment of guilt can lead the liar to make mistakes. There are two ways in which a lie is committed; conceal and falsify. When given a choice, a person will conceal rather than falsify. It is much easier to do and if caught they can explain it away. "I did not know that" or as we so often hear in court, "I have no recollection."

The best way to conceal an emotion is with a false emotion. I have been in situations that I was genuinely frightened, yet my profession dictated that I was not to show any fear. I disguised the fear with a smile. Another example is how many in the public sector see police officers as calloused because they laugh and tell jokes around horrific crime scenes. Again this is simply the police officer trying to hide in plain sight the horrific emotions that they are feeling. The smile is the most commonly used mask because the negative expressions or emotions are hard to fake.

There are two clues to deceit: leakage if the liar mistakenly reveals the clues when their behavior suggests they are lying. However, there is no specific sign of deceit. To repeat what we have already discussed, liars conceal and falsify what they expect others are going to watch the most. Liars tend to be

94

careful in their choice of words because they know that they are an expected point of deception. The second most common deception comes from the face and is the primary site to display emotions. It's the first location that everyone looks at first in another and because it's closest to the brain, the easiest to control. Recent research has shown that there is a region of the brain specifically for recognizing faces and we will start our point of attention on the right side of another's face when they are facing you.

Suspicious people should pay more attention to the voice and the body. The voice, like the face, is tied to emotions. Liars are betrayed by their words when they are careless and unprepared to tell a lie. People are also betrayed by their words through slips of the tongue. These are the Freudian slips that occur because the mind processes more words than can be told. The brain can think through almost 500 words per minute while we speak at around 125 words per minute. The third method is during outbursts when emotion overrides their common sense or preparations.

Some people show deception when they have an indirect reply to a question. The most common voice deception clues are pauses. Hesitating at the start of responding to a question or short pauses in a speech or statement can be indicative of deception. Speech errors like "aaa", "uhh", word repetitions like "I,I,I," and partial words like "rea- really" can also be indicative.

The best vocal sign of emotion is pitch. Pitch becomes higher when upset in 70% of people. Pitch will also be louder and faster when upset; slower and lower when sad.

Voice changes are hard to conceal. If you are trying to conceal fear or anger, pitch will be higher and louder and the rate, faster. Guilt can display the same as sadness. Raised pitch is not a sign of deceit, but of fear, anger, or excitement. A person who is stopped roadside by police may display a higher than normal pitch as they become scared of the questions and actions of the officer. An innocent person will generally begin to calm during the encounter.

Emblems are gestures made that have precise meaning within a culture. A shrug or giving a finger is examples. Others are head nods yes or no, hand to ear which is symbolic for louder, and a hand wave for hello or goodbye.

Emblems are always performed deliberately. Most are made out front between the waist and neck. They can be leaked or slip. One way is when only a fragment of it is performed. The other is out of the presentation position, like giving a finger when your arms are crossed. Though they slip out, they are very reliable even though neither party is aware of its presentation. They will mean exactly what is performed.

Illustrators illustrate speech as it is spoken. It is the hands that usually illustrate speech. They are used to help explain ideas that are hard to put into words or when people cannot find a word. An example is to try and explain a zig-zag. This is difficult to accomplish with a verbal explanation, yet with the use of a hand, you can make a letter "z" in the air to demonstrate. Illustrators will increase when furious, horrified, agitated, distressed or enthused.

Fewer illustrators are used if someone is not emotionally invested. If people fake enthusiasms or concern it is revealed for their lack of illustrators with their speech.

They can also decrease when someone is having a difficult time deciding what to say. They also decrease when there is caution with the speech and when someone is lying.

This is the crucial difference between emblems and illustrators. Emblems are specific in meaning and illustrators can involve a wide variety of movements. Interpreting illustrators can require previous acquaintance so a baseline is established.

Manipulators or Pacifiers are when one part of the body grooms, massages, rubs, holds, pinches, picks, scratches, or manipulates another part of the body. An increase in manipulators is a sign of anxiety, not deceit. Typically, it is the hand conducting the activity like twisting hair, finger rubs, or a foot tapped. Common recipients are the hair, ears, nose, or crotch.

Though most people are taught not to do these actions in public most are performed without self-notice. People cannot stop doing them for very long even when they try. People will look away when someone does a manipulator and look back when they are done. Fidgeting and restless movements increase when people are nervous. Body scratching, squeezing, picking, and orifice cleaning and grooming manipulators increase with discomfort.

"Any touching of the face, head, neck, shoulder, arm, hand, or leg in response to a negative stimulus (e.g., a difficult question, an embarrassing situation, or stress as a result of something heard, seen, or thought) is a pacifying behavior," according to Joe Navarro, retired FBI agent and author of numerous books and articles on body language and deception.

Men and women use the neck to pacify differently. Men are more robust, grasping, cupping, rubbing. Women are gentler, playing with a necklace or covering the suprasternal notch (the "neck dimple" below Adam's apple and above chest plate).

Touching or stroking the face, rubbing the forehead, touching, rubbing, or licking lips, pulling or massaging earlobe, stroking face or beard, playing with hair can all serve to pacify when in a stressful situation.

Careful observations are essential in watching body language. This is a system which improves with practice. But just as our systems can improve with practice, so can they atrophy without use. This is why it is so important to study as much as you can and practice what you study. Gather information from as many sources as is possible to collect on the patterns and most current directions of this science.

Autonomic nervous system clues or ANS produces noticeable changes in the body with emotional arousal like; breathing, swallowing, sweating, blushing /blanching, and pupil dilation and are involuntary when aroused. Anger increases heart rate and skin temp, and cold with fear. Raised voice pitch and louder, faster speech equates to fear, anger, and excitement.

The voice moves opposite for sad and guilt. Changes in breathing, sweating, swallowing, and dry mouth indicate strong emotions. When people lie, the "easiest to see" expressions which people pay the most attention to, are usually the false ones. It is the subtle signs that these expressions are not felt which are important and missed. Remember, these are the mask that conceals the facts.

Micro expressions flash by in less than a quarter second. They are actually full face emotional expressions that are compressed in time. The emotion may be masked with a smile, but this won't mask the emotions felt in the forehead and upper eyelids.

Crooked expressions are a clue that the feeling is not felt. They are usually stronger on the left side of the face if the person is right handed.

Expressions of long durations, 5-10 seconds, are false. Genuine emotion will not last on the face except for a few seconds. Exception is surprise.

Facial expressions not synchronized with body movements are usually deception. A real smile will raise cheeks, bagged skin below eyes, crow's feet and slight lowering of the eye brow. A fake smile only involves the movement of the mouth. Situations when detecting a lie increases when:

- Does the lie involve emotions felt at the moment? They will have to deal w/ the negative emotions of anger, fear, distress which are hard to conceal
- Is there amnesty if they confess to lying? Increases confession rates.
- High stakes of punishment or reward? Increases stressors

- Does the investigator have info that only the guilty would possess?
- Does the investigator and suspect come from the same culture and background?

Clues to Deceit

Slips of the tongue- May be emotion-specific; may leak information unrelated to emotion
Tirades- May be emotion-specific; may leak information unrelated to emotion
Indirect speech-Verbal line not prepared; or, negative emotions, most likely fear
Pauses and speech errors- Verbal line not prepared; or, negative emotions, most likely fear
Voice pitch raised- Negative emotion, probably anger and/or fear
Voice pitch lowered- Negative emotion, probably sadness
Louder, faster speech- Probably anger, fear and/or excitement
Slower, softer speech- Probably sadness and/or boredom
Emblems- May be emotion-specific; may leak information unrelated to emotion
Illustrator's decrease- Boredom; line not prepared; or, weighing each word
Manipulators increase- Negative emotion
Fast or shallow breathing- Emotion, not specific
Sweating- Emotion, not specific
Frequent swallowing- Emotion, not specific
Micro expressions- Any of the specific emotions
Squelched expressions- Specific emotion; or, may only show that some emotion was interrupted but not which one
Reliable facial muscles- Fear or sadness
Increased blinking- Emotion, not specific
Pupil dilation- Emotion, not specific
Tears- Sadness, distress, uncontrolled laughter
Facial reddening- Embarrassment, shame, or anger; maybe guilt

Facial blanching- Embarrassment, shame, or anger; maybe guilt

 With these clues in mind, let's focus on the safety concerns of fear and anger as they are signals of the arousal of emotion. The behavioral clues to these are:

Fear:
- Slips of the tongue
- Tirades
- Indirect speech
- Pauses
- Manipulators increase
- Speech errors
- Voice pitch raised
- Louder and faster speech
- Reliable facial muscles
- Facial blanching or reddening
- Increased illustrators
- Change in breathing
- Sweating
- Frequent swallowing
- Squelched expressions
- Micro expressions
- Increased blinking
- Pupil dilation

Anger:
- Slips of the tongue
- Tirades
- Voice pitch raised
- Louder and faster speech
- Emblems
- Manipulators increase
- Change in breathing
- Sweating
- Frequent swallowing
- Micro expressions

- Squelched expressions
- Increased blinking
- Pupil dilation
- Facial blanching or reddening

If at any time you are confronting another and you notice more than 1 of these actions, your awareness of safety should be on high. Fear and anger are two emotions that a person will show at a time of great consequence in their life.

Interviewing Techniques

11

In theory, there is no difference between theory and practice. But in practice, there is.

- Yogi Berra

There are many different styles of interviewing that are utilized around the world today. There is also an immense volume of research taking place each day into the various techniques believed to produce the best results. Despite what many believe, the techniques currently taught and deployed are based upon old and outdated information. It is imperative that we continually self-prepare ourselves for the ever changing world of law enforcement.

As police officers or as socially communicating people, interviewing is a learned skilled which can enhance your abilities to assimilate in society and recognize behavioral changes as they relate to deception. We have reviewed a great deal of non-verbal expressions along with their meanings. They must be examined within clusters or groups of behavior after establishing normative behavior or a baseline from which to evaluate. It is a well proven fact that your chances of recognizing deceptions are vastly improved when you focus your attention on both the verbal and non-verbal actions and reactions to a stimulus.

Current research is leading us into the direction of verbal response attention. Numerous studies show how people's verbal response to stress is generally a better indicator than non-verbal. The research into non-verbal communication is much older and far better established and excepted by most of us. It is the path which most of us spend our day's people watching while recognizing certain behaviors and most law enforcement officers possess over confidence in their abilities.

We will examine a variety of techniques which will help build the "pathway" of understanding in the final collaboration of various tried and tested interviewing tactics. To help with this sometimes confusing subject, we will explore each, where they came from, and how they apply to our learning skills. You will see as we start to conclude how parts of each will become melded together to provide a strategy to improve your skills. The techniques we are going to explore are:

- Probable Lie Comparisons (PLC)
- Statement Validity Assessments (SVA)
- Reality Monitoring (RM)
- Cognitive Interviewing Techniques
- Scan or Statement Analysis
- Assessment Criteria Indicative of Deception (ACID) – a combined research effort of the above practices

Behavior Assessment Interview

Behavioral assessment questions, also known as the "suspect elimination questions" are very effective for determining deception during the non-accusatory specific issue interview. Some of the questions are also designed to identify the most effective theme to introduce during the interrogation. They will likewise illicit fear the subject has to overcome in order to confess. These questions are completely non-accusatory and are often introduced as general or "routine" questions. It should be established at the onset of behavioral assessment questioning that "I don't know" and "I have no idea" are unacceptable answers. Explain that everybody has an opinion and surely the subject has speculated about the topic at hand. You as the investigator are merely trying to get their perspective on the case based upon their observations. Furthermore, explain that their answers are confidential and will not be shared with any other parties involved.

Before we can utilize any of the techniques, we must first be reasonably certain that we have a viable witness or suspect. One way to accomplish this is through the Behavior Assessment Interview. This is a strategy developed to illicit a response from the subject we are interviewing. The strategy includes a series of questions that when asked will bring to the forefront of their mind the topics we suspect or desire them to speak about. If they have reason to fear the topic, their responses should be greater. A guilty thinking person must have a reasonable expectation of punishment for an interview to be successful.

Therefore, these are non-accusatory and structured forensic interview questions designed to elicit verbal and nonverbal behaviors and attitudinal characteristics of the suspect being questioned. The questions asked after behavioral norms are established as either those that attempt to assess the suspect's opportunity, motivation and propensity for involvement in the issue or, are those used to elicit different verbal and nonverbal behaviors and attitudinal characteristics from truthful and deceptive persons.

In a standard interview, behavioral assessment questions are asked during the non-accusatory specific issue discussion. They can be in list form or 'peppered in' throughout the process. In a case where several individuals could have potentially committed the crime being investigated, behavioral assessment questions are used to reduce your pool of suspects. This will be demonstrated later in the section on Statement Analysis.

If being used for suspect elimination, you should pick the ten or so behavioral assessment questions to ask every subject; the same questions should be used for each subject. You will ask the questions from the list and evaluate the answers. At the end of the questions, separate and leave the opportunity for further contact open. Upon evaluating the answers, you will quickly eliminate the large majority of uninvolved subjects and identify a small group of persons that you will focus on as your core suspects. Usually, behavioral assessment questions can reduce a suspect pool by ninety percent.

Rules for evaluating behavioral assessment/suspect elimination questions:

- A guilty subjects answers will always try to broaden your investigation
- A guilty subjects answers won't logistically make sense
- A guilty subject will suggest inappropriate or mild punishments
- A guilty subject will downplay the significance of the act
- A guilty subject will downplay the impact of the act on the victim
- A guilty subject will introduce and entertain many theories as to what might have taken place, none of them will include him/her

- A guilty subject will refuse to recognize the obvious possibility of involvement
- A guilty subject will not address the question
- A guilty subject will demonstrate significant verbal and non-verbal
  Indicators of deception when answering

15 behavior provoking questions have been developed for our purposes. From these 15, they can be reworked to allow for the type of incident involved. You can reword each of these and keep them available to utilize in a specific type of investigation. In other words, develop questions for the most common types of investigation you will regularly encounter. When asking a suspect the questions, you will not want to ask every question, but choose about half to ask that could elicit the best response. The basic 15 questions as well as the reason for asking them and used in a scenario involving a theft are:

1. Purpose: What is your understanding for the purpose of this interview today?
2. You: (Name) If you stole (this money) you should tell me that now. Did you steal that money?
3. Knowledge: Do you know who stole (this money)?
4. Suspicion: Who do you suspect may have stolen (this money)?
5. Vouch: Is there anyone you can vouch for, who you do not think was involved in (this theft of money)?
6. Opportunity: Who would have had the best opportunity to (steal this money) if they wanted to?
7. Think Stolen: Do you think this (money) was actually stolen?
8. Feel: How do you feel about being interviewed regarding this (theft)?

9. Results: How do you think the investigation will come out on you?
10. Think: Have you ever thought about (stealing money)?
11. Punishment: What do you think should happen to the person who stole (this money)?
12. Second Chance: Do you think the person who (stole this money) should be given a second chance?
13. Why Not: Tell me why you wouldn't (steal this money)?
14. Motive: Why do you think someone did (steal this money)?
15. Tell Loved One: Have you told your (mother/spouse/family) about coming in for the interview today?

Another more basic format for the behavior provoking questions is:

1. Tell me whatever you have heard or know about this case?
2. Do you believe this actually happened?
3. Who do you think is responsible?
4. Any reason why somebody would think you're responsible?
5. How do you feel toward people who do these things?
6. How do you think (the victim) feels?
7. What type of person is (the victim)?
8. What should happen to the person who did this?
9. Why do you think a person would do something like this?
10. Why wouldn't you do something like this?
11. What would be your greatest concern if you failed a polygraph?

To illustrate another format for this line of questioning, the following could be used in a suspected drug stop:

1. Tell me what you know about anything illegal in the car
2. Who do you think is responsible for anything illegal in the car?
3. Is there anything illegal?
4. Is there anyone you know who would not have done this?
5. Who do you think had the best opportunity to do this?
6. How do you think this is going to turn out?
7. Have you ever thought about doing this?
8. Is there any reason why someone would have called the police to say you were transporting something illegal?
9. Tell me why you would not be involved with this.
10. How do you feel about people who transport/use?
11. Should people who do this be given a second chance?
12. How do you think the parents of the victims of this feel?
13. What do you think should happen to someone who is caught with this?
14. Why would you think someone would do this?
15. Why wouldn't you do this?

A sample behavioral assessment/suspect elimination questions for determining deception in any criminal matter would be:

Why do you think I am talking to you today?
How do you feel about being interviewed today?
Tell me whatever you have heard or know about the case?
Do you believe this actually happened?
Who do you think is responsible?
Who do you think is the least likely person responsible?
Who had the best opportunity to do this?

Any reason why someone would think you're responsible?
How do you feel toward people who do these things?
Have you ever thought about doing something like this?
How do you think the person that did this feels?
Is it possible that there is any forensic evidence in this case? (BAITING)
Would there be any reason for your (blood, semen, prints) to be found at the scene? (BAITING)
How do you think (victim) feels?
How do you think (victim) feels toward the person who did this?
What should happen to the person who did this when they are caught?
Would you give the person a second chance?
Have you talked with anybody about this case?
Did you lie to any question concerning (issue)?
During your entire life, have you ever told a serious lie to stay out of trouble?
Would you be willing to contribute money to help pay back loss just to make this thing go away?
Regarding (issue)...did you do it?

Again I should stress that it is not necessary to ask everyone all of these questions. After building some rapport with your baseline biographical questions, ask them at least 5 of these questions to see how they respond. They will be stimulated and display some type of behavioral change if they are involved in the questioned crime. It is critical to understand that each technique will not work every time. This is why it is so important to have an understanding of a variety of techniques to utilize. Everybody is different in many ways so we need to understand the differences in education, life experiences and psychological imbalances of the people we interview. Due to their upbringing; some people have been required to lie about almost everything in their life. Often these people will start to believe or confuse the truth with their lies. It can be these individuals that we will have difficulties with, but they are not impossible. The primary causes of failure by police officers to utilize the techniques is to not attempt them completely and/or being lazy in the necessary preparations to the interviews. It is human nature to find the easy way out of a situation. All of the developed programs that follow take a concerted effort, practice, and training by the officer to become efficient.

The Probable Lie Comparison (PLC) Test

This type of deceit detection testing is commonly used by polygraph examiners. It is accomplished by the use of relevant questions to specific issues as well irrelevant questions asked in a certain order or "format." This allows the examiner the opportunity to analyze how someone responds physiologically to questions by the recording of data from changes in blood pressure, heart rate, and perspiration. A relevant question is one that deals with the real issue of the investigation. These questions include asking whether the examinee perpetrated the specific act, knows who did it or is withholding known information concerning the specific issue. It can also include questions about particular pieces of evidence that could incriminate the guilty person. An irrelevant question is one designed not to invoke a response. An easy example of a comparison question would be, "Is today Monday?" Irrelevant questions are typically placed in the first position of a question list because the physiological responses that follow the appearance of the first question are presumed to have no diagnostic value. They are also placed at other points in the question sequence. Guilty examinees are expected to show stronger reactions to relevant than to control questions and no reaction to irrelevant questions; innocent examinees are expected to react similarly to both question types.

A Probable Lie Comparison (PLC) question now referred to as "Control" questions are designed to be a probable lie for the examinee. The PLC question should be similar in nature but unrelated to the specific crime or issue(s) being tested. The question should be separated from the relevant issue by time, place or category. The comparison question should use the same action verb or similar in nature action verb as that of the relevant issue. A comparison question should be broad in scope and time so that it captures as many of the examinees past life experiences as possible. An acceptable example is:

Before 1998, did you ever steal anything of value?

In the PLC format, examiners' compare responses to relevant questions with responses to control. Comparison or control questions ask about generalized acts of the type of event under investigation separated by time, place or category. In a burglary investigation, you may ask, "Prior to 2013, have you ever stolen anything of value?" In a drug related question you would ask, "Since becoming an adult, have you ever used illegal drugs?" The instructions are designed to induce innocent people to answer in the negative, even though most are lying. Innocent examinees are expected to experience concern about these answers that shows in their physiological responses. Generally, the innocent examinees will react more strongly to the comparison questions, and guilty examinees will react more strongly to relevant questions.

This occurs because an innocent examinee when asked a vague time line question like, "Have you ever used an illegal drug?" has to decide how to answer. There are many people who have never used an illicit drug yet they need to determine in their mind if they have ever used something in a way that could be seen as illicit. This can be as simple as your mother once gave you one of her prescription pills to help with a condition. Still, if you had experimented with marijuana once, 25 years ago, the examinee has to decide if they want to tell this information to the examiner. This internal struggle creates the physiological responses which will show on the testing results. They did not however, respond to the "Have you used drugs in the past year?" question because it is a present tense question. They are not using now but did use once 25 years ago. This assists the examiner in differentiating between the current deceptions from the past indiscretion.

Before starting a polygraph exam, a physical assessment of the individual can be made. I believe this is always a good idea, polygraph or not, to help show that an individual is of sound mental capacities before an interrogation. It simply helps to eliminate one of the

112

hurdles which will be attempted at a later date by the defense to show their client was not of sound mind at the time of the confession. For instance you can ask the following:

- What is your general health? Excellent, good, fair or poor. Explain.
- Have you taken any medication in the past 24 hours?
- Ask about effects of medication...You may have to go to PDR or internet.
- Alcohol in the past 24hrs?
- Are you presently being treated by a doctor? If so explain.
- Pregnancy?
- Amount of sleep in past 24 hours? What is the norm?

For the comparison questions, they must be separated from the relevant questions by time, place, or category.

- Time: Before this year...
- Place: Prior to moving to ...
- Category: Did you ever steal any Government Property (Case is theft of Private Property)

Comparison questions must be as broad in scope as possible. "Before this year, did you ever steal anything of value from your current job?"

Once we have developed our line of questioning for the style of interview we are conducting, we will follow a format. This format involves the biographical and medical assessment questions. At the same time, what we are accomplishing is the building of rapport. Rapport is always absolutely necessary to accomplish our goals. All other bias or disdain for the subject must be pushed aside to accomplish rapport. We will seek throughout the entire interview a homeostasis state for the subject. It is required to keep them on topic. When they start to veer off course or start rambling on about insignificant banter, it is your job to return them back to the topic at hand. We need to control every aspect of the interview while not appearing to do so. We can explain to them that at any time, feel free to interject and correct any information that you think is incorrect. Now that we have established a rapport and the biographical/medical assessment, we shall prepare them for the next phase.

We will ask, "I am going to ask you to be 100% truthful with me. Can you do that?" We are now ready to move to the next phase called the free narrative. They are not interrupted or challenged on the facts at this time. "Please describe everything or tell me everything you know about (the topic)?" When finished, ask clarifying questions but do not interrogate. Now we can ask a comparison – "Before today, have you ever used marijuana?" Then relevant questions like "Is there marijuana in the car?" If they become talkative about another subject stop them with a neutral question (Homeostasis) like, "What color is your car?" before asking another comparison question, "Have you ever associated with anyone who used drugs?" Follow this with another relevant question, "If it is not yours than who would have it in the car?" Once all of your questions have been exhausted you can go into a narrative review. "Let me tell you what I know so far. You are driving this car. I stopped you and smelled marijuana from inside the car. "You told me that ..." This allows them to correct anything we say that may be confusing or needs to be corrected. A simplistic example of this would be if you stopped someone for speeding or other violation and suspect them of drug smuggling. Comparison questions can lead you to an assumption one way or the other. Concern for the ticket and not drugs could show a probability of no contraband. Conversely, no concern of paying a fine could indicate contraband possession. A sample questioning may look like this:

- I am going to ask you to be 100% truthful with me, Can you do that?

114

- Free narrative – Describe everything. Tell me everything you know about this ……
- Comparison – Before today, have you ever used marijuana?
- Relevant – Are there drugs in the car?
- If they become talkative about another subject stop them with a neutral question (Homeostasis) like, "What color is your car?"
- Comparison - Have you ever associated with anyone who used drugs?
- Relevant - If it is not yours than who would have it in the car?
- Narrative Review: You are driving this car. I stopped you and smelled marijuana from inside the car. You told me that ………… Is there anything else you would like to add to prove your innocence in this matter?

If the subject is asked to assess his own level of honesty in the very beginning, the tendency is to over assess his honesty in order to add strength and credibility to his innocence. The discussion can take this direction: "How about you, in terms of honesty, how would you rate yourself personally on a scale of 1 – 100"? If the estimate is not between 95 – 100 percent continue by saying, "Really? That's kind of low. Most people are higher than that. You know yourself better than I do—give me as accurate an assessment of your honesty as you can." The subject will then give you a much higher assessment and has now committed themself to an exceptionally high degree of honesty and will become vulnerable later on when the comparison questions are established.

Close attention has to be placed on the questioning. Every word that they and you utilize counts in the determination of an answer. If you asked a question such as: "Tell me in as much detail as possible, everything you know about this event?" Look at each word used. You did not ask them for a definitive answer, just what could be possible to tell me now. The word "possible" translates to likely, probable, or potential. You have given them a way out of the question. A better question is: "I need you to tell me everything that you know about this…" or "everything that occurred from the time you arrived at work to the time you left on ………." Or "Explain everything without leaving out even the smallest detail of your entire day on …….. This type of word analysis will be discussed further in the section on Statement Analysis.

Some examples of irrelevant or comparison would be:
- During the first (DTF) _____ years of your life do you remember (DYR) stealing?
- DTF _____ years of your life DYR cheating?
- DTF _____ years of your life DRY lying?
- DTF _____ years of your life DRY using illegal drugs?

Below is a list of irrelevant or comparison questions you could ask in a drug investigation.
- Did you ever do anything you could be arrested for?
- Did you ever do anything against the law?
- Did you ever lie to anyone about using drugs?
- Did you ever use any drugs illegally?
- Did you ever think of using any illegal drugs?
- Have you used any narcotics since you got out of jail?
- Did you smoke marijuana more than ___ times? (Use the number of times the subject admits.)
- Did you use any narcotics since_____? (Date admitted last used.)
- Did you ever get sick from using drugs?
- Did you ever get "high" from using drugs?
- Did you ever miss work because of using drugs'?
- Did you ever take any medication without a doctor's OK?
- Did you ever smoke anything containing a drug?
- Did you ever inhale anything containing a drug?

- Did you ever smoke marijuana?
- Did you ever use any narcotics?
- Have you used narcotics more than _____ times? (Use the number of times subject admits.)
- Have-you used any drugs since you've been on parole? (probation)
- DYR ever being more involved with drugs than what you told me?
- DYR ever dealing drugs for a profit?

These are some sample comparison questions you could use in a drug investigation. Create a list of the most common types of investigations you conduct each year. Draft a list of comparison and relevant questions that apply to the subject matter. Once completed, you can use the list to effectively inquire about their involvement without the need of creating a new list before each scenario. You have removed much of the needed preparation required to effectively initiate and conduct an interview by streamlining the process and preventing ineffective "off the cuff" questioning.

Statement Validity Assessments

Statement Validity Assessment (SVA) is the technique most widely used for determining the truthfulness of verbal statements. It was first developed in Germany in the 1950's for use on minors who were victims of sexual abuse. This was conducted because the testimony of minors could not always be considered dependable. The children were too susceptible to outside influences. This type of testing assist in determining testimony based on a real experience because it differs in quality and content from an imagined event.
SVA is made up of three mutually dependent components:

   a) A structured interview with the victim.
   b) Criteria-Based Content Analysis or CBCA, which assesses the content of the person's testimony.
   c) The integration of CBCA with the information obtained through a set of questions called the Validity Checklist.

In order to accomplish the structured interview have the subject talk at least 95% of the time. All too often interviewer's talk too much which allows the suspect to gather information and tell you information based around your wording. In other words, we are telling or feeding them what to say. This is one of several types of influences adults can have on children. We learned to be cognizant of our word usage in the Probable Lie Comparison (PLC) section because adults are listening to your words for clues how to best answer the questions. To accomplish this use open ended questioning styles.

As for the Criteria-Based Content Analysis or CBCA, this is accomplished via a 19 question test analysis of the content of the person's testimony. This question criterion consists of the following questions and categories:

General Characteristics:
    1. Logical structure
    2. Unstructured production
    3. Quantity of details
Specific Content:
    4. Contextual embedding – events are placed in time and location
    5. Description of interactions – I ran left and he approached from the other side.
    6. Reproduction of conversation
    7. Unexpected complications during the incident
Peculiarities of Content:
    8. Unusual details
    9. Superfluous details – unrelated, I was watching Family Fued when I heard ….
    10. Accurately reported details misunderstood
    11. Related external associations
    12. Allusions to subjective mental state
    13. Attribution of the accused's mental state
Motivation-Related Content:
    14. Spontaneous corrections
    15. Admitting lack of memory
    16. Raising doubts about one's own testimony
    17. Self-Deprecation – humor about something negative
    18. Pardoning the accused
Specific Elements of the Offence:
    19. Specific details of the offence

The SVA process begins with the interview. As always, the interviewer must have some preparatory time to develop the theme of questions based upon the criteria. To do this, the interviewer has to be familiar with the content of the case as well as the test criteria. CBCA will be influenced by what the subject has or has not experienced. Therefore the interviewer must also take into consideration the biographical background of the subject as well as the person's age, experience and cognitive ability level during rapport building. The verbal content of the statement is analyzed through the application of the 19 criteria, organized in five broad categories, and with the purpose of differentiating between true and fabricated statements. The basic idea is that a true testimony contains a greater number of criteria. However, there is no minimal score, yet the higher the score the more valid.

The development and testing of SVA was groundbreaking and found to be highly effective with juvenile victims and witnesses. Researchers then began the testing of these processes with adults. The foundation of the testing was the same except for a reduction of CBCA criteria questions. Research found that the criteria questioning could be reduced. The following are believed to be the 14 most effective questions:

1. False statements have few details or an unusually large number of details. True statements have many details or unusual details related to the event.

    "The man had a strange odor."
    "She screamed real loud before she hit me."

2. Superfluous details unrelated to the event.

    "I had been watching Americas Funniest Videos that morning so I was in a good mood."
    "I had been to McDonalds that morning and they forgot to give me   a straw."

3. Contextual embedding - Events are placed in time and location. Actions are connected with other daily activities.

    "I was passing the Publix when I heard the gunshot."
    "I was watching the news, which I always do at 6:00 p.m., when I heard a loud scream."

4. Descriptions of Interactions - Action of A - Reaction of B - Reaction of A

    "I moved toward the door, he stepped in front of me, I ran the other way."

"He glared at me, I glared back, he started to smile."

"I left him a message, he didn't call back, I called him again."

Deceptive statements are often general

"I ran out the back."

"We stared at each other."

"He never called me back."

5. Reproduction of Conversation

Truthful Statement:

I said. "We should see other people." She replied that, "She would not let that happen."

I asked her why she was lying. She said that she wasn't lying, and I said, "Yes you are."

Deceptive Statements of the same conversation:

"We discussed our relationship."

"She denied that she was lying."

True Statements possess:

6. Unusual details – tattoos, stutters, quirks

7. Spontaneous Corrections

8. Admitting Lack of Memory

9. Raising Doubts about One's Own Testimony

10. Self-Deprecation

11. Pardoning the Perpetrator

12. Subjective Mental State

Describes feelings or thoughts

"I was very scared."

"Her actions made me nervous."

"I felt humiliated."

"He made me so angry."

13. Attribution of Perpetrator's Mental State - Describes the perpetrator's feelings or thoughts experienced at the time of the incident.

"You could see in his eyes how angry he was."

"The way he held his head let you know that he thought he was in control."

"She seemed confused and perhaps a bit guilty about what she was doing."
14. Clarity
  False statements:
    Don't make sense
  True statements:
    Have a logical structure
    Contain details characteristic of the offense
    Are told with an appropriate affect
    Are consistent with other statements
    Are consistent with other evidence

The third component of the process is the integration of CBCA with the information obtained through a set of categories called the Validity Checklist. The Validity Checklist is made up of four general categories of information:

a) Psychological characteristics - In this category it is important to assess the appropriateness of language, affect and susceptibility to suggestion.

b) Interview characteristics - Analyze the quality of the interview rating the type of questions asked such as are they suggestive, leading or coactive and their overall appropriateness to the situation.

c) Motivation for making false accusations - The information in this category should help to rule out those aspects that may be influencing the person to provide a false testimony. It should also be understood that a minor can be under pressure from a third person to make a false statement. An important aspect of this category is the context in which the statement is generated.

d) Aspects related to the investigation - This section is designed with the aim of rating the consistency between previous statements and investigation results.

Reality Monitoring

Reality Monitoring identifies memories originating from true experiences and should include more perceptual information (visual details, sounds, smells, tastes and physical feelings related to the event), contextual information (information regarding when and where the event happened), and affective information (details of feelings about thoughts, reasoning, and inferences of events) than memories based on fabrication. This style of interviewing is easier to learn than Statement Validity Analysis or SVA because the questioning is directed towards these specific areas.

The testimony or statement is examined for full sensory representation. Liars tend to talk in the abstract or brief summary rather than complete details. They are likely to make use of audio/visual descriptions that are free of sensory detail. Truth tellers are more likely to add sensory-based detail. Reality monitoring scores the records of interviews along the following dimensions:

- Visual details or descriptions of what the person saw: "I saw that the car was missing."
- Auditory details or descriptions of what was heard: "I heard the screen door slam."
- Spatial details, where the event took place: "I went across the street to Joe's house."
- How objects are arranged in space: "I heard sounds coming from above me."
- Temporal details, how things are arranged in time and how long they lasted: "First, I knocked on the door. Then, I looked in the window. Finally, I let myself in." "I was only there for about five minutes but it seemed like an hour."

Like the CBCA analysis, reality monitoring is usually conducted with a written transcript of the interview. It is scored so that the more the sensory elements appear; the greater the likelihood is that the speaker is telling the truth. Reality monitoring contrasts the characteristics of a full sensory representation of a real event, with the basics of a fabricated story. When lies are presented as truth, the speaker is often unwilling to acknowledge mistakes. Someone trying to deceive will try to stay on a "lie script." This is a prepared idea of how the events took place. It is too difficult to create all of the sensory recognitions to these stories so there are few details and personal narratives included. The lie must be presented as practiced and attempts to access details out of order may increase signs of nervousness.

In contrast, the truth is rich in personal insights and sensory details. A truth teller understands that they may not get it right completely and is willing to make adjustments to the story line. They often ramble and go off track and include details that are irrelevant to the problem at hand. This process is impossible to the deceiver because to change course in their story means leaving the "lie script" and this creates cognitive overload.

The key to lie detection for these methods is to keep track of behavioral details instead of trying to determine whether the speaker was lying. This equates to the need to have the statement in writing. We can then study this statement word for word and keep track of these required details. This will give us the groundwork needed to explain how we understand that the statement is false. Again, the central task is not trying to determine who is lying, but just keeping track of the details. These details show us who the truth tellers are. Some of the key details found were:

1. The lag time between the question and the answer (increased for liars)
2. Hand and finger movements without moving the arms (decreased for liars)
3. Speech hesitations: "uhs," "ums," or "aahs" between words (increased for liars)
4. The quantity and specificity of details (decreased for liars)
5. Descriptions of time and location (decreased for liars)

6.   The reproduction of conversation (decreased for liars)
7.   Descriptions of other people's feelings, thoughts, or motives (decreased for liars);
8.   The inclusion of visual and auditory details (decreased for liars)
9.   The inclusion of spatial (where) information and temporal (time) details (decreased for liars)

Cognitive Interviewing Techniques (CI)

The Cognitive Interviewing Technique was developed by Dr. Edward Geiselman (UCLA) and Dr. Ron Fisher (FIU). The standard Cognitive Interviewing (CI) process is a 6-step procedure to enhance memories of witnesses and victims. It has been shown to increase detection of deception by 25-40%.

A common problem which an investigator encounters is when the witnesses or victims "cannot remember" certain events. This has been found not to be a result of not witnessing but rather an inability to remember. When we are faced with a situation perceived by the brain as threatening, the brain focuses all of our sensory receptors to the threat in an effort of self-preservation. Because of this focus, we will not remember certain occurrences within an event. The Cognitive Interviewing Technique has been developed to help investigators retrieve this stored information. The steps to this process are as follows:

Step 1 – Introduction / Rapport – Discuss with the subject neutral topics or even topics of shared interest for which they have no reason to lie.

Step 2 - Narrative – Instruct them to tell everything about the event including the smallest of details. As seen, people have a natural habit of editing information. We may not intend to deceive in any way but it takes too long to explain every detail. We want them to return to the scene mentally and relive the before, during, and after events. We should not challenge any statements but extenders are alright. (What happened then?)

Step 3 - Sketch – Ask them to draw a sketch or illustration of the event like the general layout of the area where the incident occurred and then trace the events as they unfolded from start to finish.

Step 4 - Follow-up – Ask open ended questions which will further the clarification w/o confrontation and locks them into the statement.

Steps 5 - Reverse order – When all of the scenes of the narrative are completed with the above steps, ask them to describe the event again but in reverse order; ending to start.

Step 6 - Challenge – Remaining soft spoken and respectful ask them about any inconsistencies or incriminating statements. It is alright to even tell them that you believe they are lying about the entire event.

One of the most important issues in CI is that the interviewer remains silent while the interviewee recalls the experience. However much an interviewee appears to be drifting into irrelevancies, they should remain uninterrupted.

The interviewee must be encouraged to recall the experience without the normal editing of social conversation. Rapport is essential and the interviewer needs to put the interviewee at ease and give them latitude to tell their story in detail. We need to be very attentive to what the interviewee is saying without note taking. This attentiveness and freedom from interruption seems to encourage interviewees to provide numerous details to serve as affirmation the belief that they are being taken seriously. They can be placed into such a detailed recall that incidents lasting minutes are recalled in hours.

The main techniques employed to enhance recall is 'context reinstatement'. The purpose is to return the interviewee in their mind to the context in which the experience occurred. Often this entails no more than asking the interviewee to relax, possibly to close their eyes, and recall where and when the incident occurred. They should be encouraged to recall the scene and in their mind to look around it and note who was present, what they could see, hear, touch and smell. They might be asked to remember what had happened immediately prior to the incident. It can be valuable to ask the interviewee to draw a map of the location and indicate where others were standing, sitting, etc. However achieved, it is important to awaken the interviewee's memory of the context and they should be allowed time to do so. The context cues will then assist recall.

The interviewee is then invited to recount their experience in whatever way they choose. Narrative is the most common structure, but some may begin by recalling the most memorable feature of the experience. Not until they have fully completed this initial recall does the interviewer intervene. There may be elements of the account that fail to connect, e.g. the interviewee has failed to acknowledge that they moved from one location to another, or left unexplained what prompted some specific course of action. The interviewer now invites them to return to each significant moment in turn, reinstating the context each time (paying as much attention to doing so as they did initially) and asks the interviewee to elaborate.

Once the interviewee appears to have recalled as much as possible, it may prove beneficial to use other techniques to unlock their memory. First, we will ask them to reverse the narrative; to ask them to recall what happened immediately prior to some particularly important moment, e.g. what occurred immediately before an eruption of violence. This inhibits interviewees from skipping over steps in the narrative because they are taken for granted. The most important prelude to each exploration of detail must be to reinstate the context and definitely not to rush them into providing an account. The interview may end with the interviewer giving the subject challenge questions to clarify any issues that exist.

An audio recording of the interview is essential because of the large amount of data produced by the recall. A transcript of the interview can be useful in placing the various recalled events of various orders into a useful arrangement of subject matter, e.g. descriptions of people that may be scattered throughout the interview can be brought together. It can be made useful to the investigator if the transcripts are also collected in an understandable order and scribed in the third person vocabulary. If possible, this investigative composite of the interview can be presented to the interviewee for amendment and endorsement.

When revealing the differences between truthful and deceptive subjects, the following was found.

- Narratives offered were significantly longer by the truthful.
- Drawing task deceptive - Time consuming and failure to include narrative elements, starting over because of inconsistencies, changing or correcting elements of the story and needed the most time to complete.
- Truthful drawing task added new consistent details.
- Truthful follow ups took longer because of all of the detail.
- Deceptive reverse order stories needed prompts not to significantly leap back in time and reverting to forward recalling details.
- When asked to clarify unresolved inconsistencies, truthful people often explained due to miss communication (let me explain, I wasn't clear before) while deceptive people has a claim of memory (I was mistaken; it was this way)
- When asked if they wanted to add anything, deceptive persons would quickly say no, while truthful persons would elaborate or hesitate before a no.
- When challenged about lying, deceptive persons would look unhappy or uncomfortable, then offer weak denials or deflect the challenge. Truthful people would offer a firm denial of lying and offer additional info to support their position.

There were three major deception indicators prevalent especially during the drawing, reverse order and challenge phase. One is that people trying to deceive tell unnatural stories. These stories have few details, end abruptly, has contradictions, lack chronology, possess vague or an illogical story line, and had awkward use of terms. The second is exaggerated behavior which includes inappropriate smiling, shrugging, grooming, and rationalizing. The third is unusual eye contact or movements which included blinking, squinting, exaggerated movements, and looking down or around the room.

As has been the rule of understanding from the beginning and is always worth repeating throughout, everything has to be taken into clusters. Dr. Geiselman was quoted as saying, "Detection of any one indicator should not be taken as sufficient evidence to conclude that the subject is being deceptive. Instead, judgments must be based on the overall pattern of performance through the entire CI protocol."

Statement Analysis (SA) or SCAN Analysis (Scientific Content Analysis)

When trying to detect a lie without equipment like a polygraph or voice analysis, you are left to three options:
Statement Analysis
Body language
Handwriting

Scan Analysis is the process of analyzing a person's words to determine if they are being truthful or deceptive. People will always word their statement based on their knowledge acquired through life experience and education. Therefore, their statement may include information they did not intend to share with you. This will be done without their realization of the degree of leakage provided. It is nearly impossible to give a lengthy deceptive statement without revealing it as a lie. These techniques are very accurate because they are based on the English language specifically word definitions and the rules of grammar.

Statement Analysis, or Scientific Content Analysis (SCAN), examines open ended written accounts in which the writers choose where to begin and what to include in the statements. It was created by Avinoam Sapir, who developed this technique based upon thousands of interviews he conducted as a Police Lieutenant and polygraph examiner in the Israeli Police. According to Sapir, "when people are given the choice to give their own explanation in their own words, they would choose to be truthful . . . . It is very difficult to lie with commitment."

According to an analysis of the SCAN technique in 2001, the report said SCAN "claims to be able to detect instances of potential deception within the language behavior of an individual; it does not claim to identify whether the suspect is lying." The goal is to highlight areas of a text that require clarification as part of an interview strategy.

131

We use words to define our reality. When we lie, we're trying to adjust two things in our minds at the same time: the real events and the invented or disguised version of them. The language we use reflects that tension and when it does, the language we use does not follow our normal patterns. Most deceptive stories (80%-90%) push the main issue of the statement to the end and does not continue the narrative afterwards. They end abruptly or not at all, as if they did not want to tell the big lie and waited as long as possible. With these facts in mind, it is imperative and repeatable to understand that people mean what they say. It does not mean that they are lying, but people have a tendency to only say part of the entire story. As already understood, no person recites every detail of anything they have experienced. It takes too long. We all "edit" in that we tell only what we think is important to include in a statement. We also do this in conversation. SCAN or SA takes into consideration only the words used by the person. What the subject does while talking (including body language), what the subject implies, what the listener/reader knows, does not play a role in the analysis.

SCAN/SA can be applied anywhere there is an "open statement," in which the subject can say anything he wants. President Clinton said, "I was bound to be truthful and I tried to be." By using the word "tried" indicates that he attempted to be truthful, but failed. When a rape victim uses the pronoun "we" in her statement she is revealing she is being deceptive. The pronoun "we" not only shows plurality but it also means a partnership was formed. We would not expect a rape victim to partner up with her attacker. When a person uses phrases such as "later on" or "afterwards" he has withheld some information by skipping over something in his story. A man when accused of rape said, "I categorically deny these charges and intend to vigorously defend myself against these allegations."

"Deny" can mean refute or refusal to take responsibility. The word "intend" means 'have in mind or

132

to plan.' He did not say he will defend himself, only to consider it.

Grammar like recalling something that has happened should be in past tense. If lying, they will not be able to use the past tense because they have no memory of the event.

Another example of using the rules of grammar to detect deception is how a person uses articles within their statement. When we introduce someone or something that is unknown, we are required to use the indefinite articles "a" or "an." Once the introduction has been made, we then use the definite article "the." We see this in the following statement:

"A man approached me and pointed a gun at me. He stuck the gun in my ribs and forced me into the car."

In the first sentence, the victim properly refers to the attacker and the weapon as "a man" and "a gun." Once the victim identifies the gun, he then correctly refers to it as "the gun" in the second sentence. A problem arises when he refers to the vehicle as "the car." Since this is the first time he mentions the vehicle, he should have called it "a car." Using the article "the" tells us the victim either recognized the car or he is making up the story. Since he was thinking to place a car into the story, his mind had already introduced the car.

Many times the truth goes unnoticed because people like to interpret what a person has said. However, you should never interpret but take the words at face value. Remember, people mean exactly what they are saying. Generally, people do not want to lie. Even hard core criminals do not want to lie because they are unsure to the facts that the police have in the case. The best way to handle this is with a truthful statement with specific facts left out. A "yes or no" question has to be answered with a "yes or no" answer. "Never" cannot be used in place of "no." When asked a direct question such as, "Did you do it?" They will answer "never" which is a denial. Another example would be if asked, "Did you take the money?" "I never took the money" instead of "No, I did not take the money" is indicative of deception.

When asked if she would run for President, Condoleezza Rice said, "I have never wanted to run for anything." Though a good political position, a "yes" would have caused a stir and a "no" would have canceled future hopes.

When a FBI agent was asked a question which involves helping a mobster, "Did you go over the line?" he answered, "Anyone in my business that knows what they are doing, knows enough to walk up to that line, but to never step over it." His answer was a statement that we appreciate, but it did not answer the question.
"And you didn't?" he was asked.
"I never stepped over the line."
He was unable to say "no".
"Never" has meaning and can be used. It means not ever. When asked "have you ever?" never is alright.
"Have you ever been to –?" "Never."
"Have you been too –?" "No."
Bill Clinton was asked, "Have you ever used illegal drugs?"
Clinton responded - "I have never broken the laws of my country."
The interviewer recognized he had not answered the question, but had given an answer, "my country," which leads to a good follow up question. "Alright how about the laws of another country or have you used illegal drugs?" When asked this more direct question, Bill Clinton had to say that he had smoked marijuana while in England. Always listen for the word "never" and decide if the person has used it correctly.

You can only believe what they have told us. Do not try to assume anything. Subject matters can be connected together with an "and". Confessions can be found by examining pronouns because they show responsibility. "You know" is often used by people because they want you to take for granted what they are saying as the truth.

Everyone has their own choice of words, for example gun instead of pistol. In statement analysis there are no synonyms. Every word has a meaning. Statements can be examined for deception by examining their personal dictionary. Consistency is imperative. A story with a car has to stay a car and not switch to a vehicle.

When talking about a shooting incident an officer may say "I drew my gun. I pointed my gun. I fired my weapon and holstered the gun." This says his personal dictionary is a gun when not firing, a weapon when it is being fired.

Another example of word consistency is:

"At the end of the day I counted the currency that was in my drawer. I wrote down the total amount and then counted it a second time as is our practice. I placed the currency in a bag and recorded the total amount. I then put the money in the safe."

For bank employees it is common to use the word currency. Money is a common word used when the currency becomes your property.

Not answering the question asked could be a sign of deception.

Timothy McVeigh was asked "Did you do it?"

With his attorney present he said, "The only way we can answer that is that we are going to plead not guilty."

He did not answer the question. "We" implied him and his attorney. "Really" means, truly or genuinely, so it is the only way he can answer. He cannot say "No, I didn't do it."

Later he was asked "Have you ever built a bomb?"

"I've never had my hand on a bomb."

Never is used instead of no, but the question used the word ever. Having been in the military he surely has touched a hand grenade. What should you do if the person does not answer the question directly? Ask the same question again and again until they answer. Not answering specific questions is a favorite tactic of people. You must listen so you can repeat the question until they answer specifically as asked.

When someone answers a question with a question this is because of a sensitive topic. They are hoping you will accept their answer and forget the original question. This is a commonly utilized deception we see even today as multiple scandals are occurring within various branches of our government. The House and Senate members asking questions which witnesses avoid. To our dismay, congressional members are poor interviewers and the people answering are nowhere near to responding to the questions asked. They misdirect and explain away nothing with the hopes that if they explain nothing long enough, it will be interpreted as a legitimate answer and the proceedings will close without answers. Some watching these debacles has referred to this as verbal confetti.

"Did you take the money?"

"Did I take the money? No."

He answered but he delayed the question to think how he should answer it. When asked, "Did you take the money? No." They are not looking for an answer because they already know and respond without hesitation.

"I would not do that" while often taken as a denial, is not a denial of past activity. It is a statement of future intent, telling us what the subject would not do. This is not the same as "I did not do that."

"I would like to assure the world that I did not plan the recent attacks, which seems to have been planned by people for personal reasons," bin Laden's statement said. "I would like to assure you"...is not the same as "I assure you that..." The subject is only saying what he would like to do but he is not saying what he actually does.

As observed, this process is best conducted in a written statement. We can provide the interviewee with the paper and pen and ask them to write everything that occurred with the event in question. If you have not received a written statement, a transcribed audio recording will also work. Instead of a focused and limited question and answer session, you simply let the subject describe in their own words what happened during the day of the event and write it down or otherwise record the statement. The interviewee is asked to describe the event in question from their perspective. By letting them express the complete day in detail, you develop a complete accounting in their words without any questioning from yourself. Pointed and focused questions can be used after this technique is first employed. We are going to be focusing on the following word analysis.

Pronoun Analysis

Pronouns are parts of speech that take the place of nouns. Subject pronouns include I, you, he, she, it, they, we. Object pronouns include me, you, him, her, it, us, and them. Possessive pronouns show who owns something described in a sentence. They include mine, his, hers, its, ours, yours, their, and theirs.

The best way to define the words is to examine the statement and determine the normative use. Whenever the pronoun "I" is used repeatedly and then shifts to some other pronoun such as "we," this area needs to be explored. The pronoun "I" needs to be given special focus in the statement. Most people will reply in the first person "I". Any deviation from that would be a subconscious indicator and red flag of deception. "What did you do?" or "What happened?" questions should be answered starting with "I". Not using it shows the speaker is not committed to the statement. Without the "I" you cannot believe the person has done what he claims and if they overuse "I" then this shows the person is tense and possibly deceptive. When someone answers a question untruthfully concerning themselves, they may subconsciously attempt to draw focus away by avoiding the use of the first person pronoun "I". This could include words such as "we", "they", "them", "the other", or even "it." One of the best indicators is a statement in which the subject continues to describe their accountings using the word "I" before suddenly changing. An example of this is:

"I woke up this morning at 6:00am. I got up and made coffee. I ate breakfast and then I got ready to leave for the day. After putting on my tie, I left at almost 9:00. Drove to the office and worked until 5:00."

In the above statement, we can see how the writer uses "I" continuously until he arrives at work. We are not told what time he arrived or what happened during his time at the office. He is specific until after leaving his house. The remainder of the time frame is vague until it is time to go home.

The same situation arises any time the pronoun "we" is used when the first person pronoun "I" is appropriate. The "I" pronoun is the norm for most statements. The subject's subconscious is at work attempting to distance them by having others involved when there is no one else. Another concern is when people will subconsciously shift from one pronoun to another in events when they are trying to account for specific descriptions. For example:

"The work day was over about 9:00 PM and they left to go to the Pub. It was late, but they wanted to go for drinks. Once we left the Pub........"

Notice the shift from "they" to "we." Possessive pronouns work the same way as pronouns when describing people. Just like the deviation of "we" to "they", a sudden switch in the use of possessive pronouns should cause a concern. For example,

"We took our money and went down to the corner store. We parked on Main Street because we could not find a close place to park. We then walked down about two blocks and turned right onto 5th with our money. They hit John over the head and took the money."

The writer uses the pronoun "we" until the story arrives at the critical point of the attack and then switches to "they". In addition, notice each statement included "our money" until the event occurred. At the time of the event, "our money" becomes "the money". The writer is trying to distance themselves from the events.

We will also seek the shortest route of communication as a norm. If a statement starts and carries through with a phrase like "My wife and I" each and every time, this should be examined closer. After the first use of the phrase, you have introduced the two of you as together and it would become more appropriate to use the word "we" from there on out.

Examine this statement for possessive pronouns by a subject whose house has burned down.

"I left my house right after breakfast to join my friends at the track for the day.... I drove back to my house, made a few phone calls, then went out to dinner with Stan Thompson.... Stan dropped me off at my house around 10:00. After I changed my clothes I left the house to spend the night at my cousin Tom's. Around midnight we heard fire engines and got up to see what was going on."

The house was his (my house) until the time of the fire and he distanced himself by changing the possessive pronoun "my" to "the."

Noun Analysis

Nouns denote persons, places, and things. Yet, nouns take on different meanings, depending on the individual. When examining the words used by a suspect, you should be aware of any changes, because a "change of language reflects a change in reality." Noun analysis examines the statement for any change in the noun used in the description. An example might look something like this...

"My wife and I left the house about 7:30 and went to the Marina. My wife and I left the Marina in our boat at about 9:00 AM. We obtained fuel and food in the boat store and then my wife and I headed for Creek Cove. Arriving at about 10:15, the boat was anchored and my wife and I started to swim. I got back out of the water about 10:30. It was about 10:45 when I noticed that Cindy was not in sight."

Notice the change from "wife" to 'Cindy." He has removed the possessive family relationship noun of "my wife" to the less personal noun of her name "Cindy."

Verb Analysis

Verbs will generally express action in the subject's accounting of events and will be stated in a tense form. Tense in action is stated in either past, present or future. Anytime the tense in a statement changes, this is an area of caution. When someone is telling about an event which is true and occurred to them, it has to be told in past tense. The events have already occurred and they are simply re-telling them. If the story is replaced with present tense words, you have to question the validity of the statement. Here is an example of this:

"About the middle of last month, I went down to the airport to wash my plane. I parked in the normal member's only area. I approached the hanger door. Opening the door, I see that my plane is gone. I went up to the office and asked if anyone knew anything about the plane. I then called the police."

Notice that the subject switched from past tense to present tense when he opened the door and noted that his plane was not in the hanger. He then switched back to past tense. This is often done in a subconscious manner and is indicative that this portion of the statement should be considered suspicious.

Chronology of Events

In witness statement analysis, there can be many signs of unnecessary information and information presented out of order in relationship to time. These indicators should be considered suspicious. When a truthful person describes events for a day, those events are usually set out in a chronological way. The person lived the events and will explain them as they were experienced. They may even make self-corrections on minor details in order to maintain this order. This shows that the events did occur and they are not speaking from a "lie script." When the account is not presented in a chronological manner, it is disorganized and uncharacteristic with a truthful statement and a cause for concern.

A justification to action is another red flag. It's an opinion. Remember, you didn't ask for opinion or justification, just facts set out in the subjects own words. This extra information should be viewed with suspicion. The more disorganized an account, the more the account is out of order chronologically and the more extraneous information is found in an account, the more the account becomes suspect.

Qualifying Statements

Unnecessary phrases are what a subject adds to an accounting of events. This indicates they have no conviction to the topic. The subject will sometimes conceal this lack of conviction with language indicating that they cannot remember. A person engaged in deception is more likely to use extraneous phrasing such as "I believe, I think or kind of or to the best of my knowledge." These phrases are concerns because they demonstrate their refusal to commit to the story. Examples of this are if someone should be scared and it's described as, "kind of" or if someone should be mad and it's described as, "I think I was."

Balance Testing

Sometimes caution can be drawn from considering the total content of the statement details. Application of a balance test to the statement can demonstrate deception. A statement should have three parts:

1) Accounting leading up to event.
2) Accounting of the actual event
3) Accounting of what happened after the event

Checking the balance of a statement is done by counting the total number of lines in the open statement, then dividing it into the three different sections (prior, during, and after). A general rule to follow when analyzing statements is to look for an even distribution of time in the statement. Many statements will have approximately three lines per hour of time throughout the subject's day. When this balance is severely skewed, it is an important signal.

A written statement should not be done on a computer, as a grammar/spell checker will alter the statement and we seek the subject's own words, not those that are grammatically correct. "Every person has his own linguistic code. By using linguistic methods to break and decipher the subject's linguistic code, we are able to obtain more information and to reach an accurate decision concerning the reliability of the information," according to Mr. Sapir.

In a SCAN Analysis we are seeking signs of deception, accuracy or editing: The story behind the story. The technique deals only with activities and not with intentions. Analysis does not deal with what people did, but with what people said that they did. The technique examines written statements and divides them into three main categories: before, during, and after the act under investigation. A SCAN report is not evidence to be admitted as an exhibit in court. It is a tool to help you obtain and evaluate information.

In addition to the SCAN process, a set of ten questions (Behavior Analysis) were developed to assist in determining the truthful persons when multiple suspects existed. It is called the VIEW or Statement Questionnaire. This set of questions are written and issued to the subjects under investigation and it is designed to focus the investigation based solely on the analysis of what was written. It has also been called the SCAN questionnaire. They follow along four types of questions. Open questions to obtain information, specific questions to force the guilty to lie, projective questions to assess verbal clues, and post interview questions to help identify the truthful persons.

Instructions:
Every word is important and may be checked later on
There is only one chance to write your answers so be sure to think about how you are going to phrase the answers.
Please write your answers as detailed as you can to enable us to understand your answers.
Use pen only, no pencils or typing is allowed.
Write in clear handwriting in order for us to understand them.
You are not to make any corrections. If you feel you need to make a correction, circle the words you would like to change and then write in your correction which will be taken into consideration.

Page 2 – We have reached the conclusion that something has taken place (theft of money, property, etc.). How would you explain this? Please write in detail your ideas that would account for this.

Page 3 – If you were going to conduct the investigation, how would you do it?

Page 4 – List the five most important causes that have created this situation.

Page 5 – Describe in detail your work day on (date), covering the time you came into work until the time you ended your day or your entire day from waking to sleep.

Page 6 – A) It does not mean you are right and whatever you say is confidential, if you had to suspect someone of doing this, who would you suspect and why?
B) Who would you least suspect and why?
C) What do you think should happen to the person that did this when they are caught?
D) Would you give them a second chance?
E) Do you believe this was deliberate or an accident?

Page 7 – Do you know for sure who did this?
A) Did you do this?
B) How do you think the investigation will turn out concerning you, and whether you did this?

Page 8 – Would you like to change any of the information that you gave us?
A) Is there anything we did not ask you about this that you think is important for us to know?

Page 9 – Post Interview – How do you feel now that you have completed the form?
A) Should we believe your answers?
B) If your answer to the last question is yes, give us one reason why?
C) What would you say if it was later determined you lied on this form?
D) What were your emotions while filling out the form?
E) Were you afraid?
F) If you were asked to pay for _____ how much would you be willing to pay?

To evaluate the questionnaire, the last page, post-interview is reviewed first. If the subject answered "yes" to question A (Should we believe your answers?) and then answered any other question with:
    I told the truth.
    I did not lie
    I did not do the crime
Then the suspect is placed in the truthful group. All others are attached to the problem group.

For the problem group, the questionnaire is reissued except with a change to question 2 – We have reached the conclusion you have not told us everything you know about the (crime). How would you explain this? Please write in detail your ideas that would account for this. Having to answer the questionnaire is irritating to truthful persons, and they are more likely to answer question A part 9 on the last page that we should believe their answers and allow themselves to be eliminated by answering at least one of the other questions with:

    I told the truth.

    I did not lie

    I did not do the crime

It is also important to see if there is a strong focus of the group to blame someone for the crime and also eliminate a person.

Scenario –

Page 2 – Miscount or misplaced, I can see missing one day and find the next.

3 – More attention downstairs, people watching the door more closely.

4 – Watching the door, check for alarms, check in and out.

5 – Do you know who took – no

Did you – No, of course no

Who do you suspect – no one

Who would you least suspect – everyone the same

What should happen to them – the boss's job

Second chance – bosses job

Any reason evidence turn up against you – I don't think so

Stolen or misplaced – misplaced or stolen by customers

How do you feel – sad

Should we believe you - it depends on you, your opinion

If yes why – because this is my answer

What if it turned out it was you – no reason to believe this

In their study entitled, Verification and Implementation of Language-Based Deception (2008),

Bachenko, Fitzpatrick, and Schonwetter, sought out information which differentiates the areas of a statement that could be deceptive instead of classifying an entire statement as deceptive. They stated, "Our research on deception detection differs from most previous work in two important ways. First, we analyze naturally occurring data, i.e. actual civil and criminal narratives instead of laboratory generated data. Second, we focus on the classification of specific statements within a narrative rather than characterizing an entire narrative or speaker as truthful or deceptive. We assume the authors of the statements are neither always truthful nor always deceptive. Rather, every narrative consists of declarations, or assertions of fact, that retain a constant value of truth or falsehood."

Features of narrative structure and length, text coherence, factual and sensory detail, filled pauses, syntactic structure choice, verbal immediacy, negative expressions, tentative constructions, referential expressions, and particular phrasings have all been shown to differentiate truthful from deceptive statements in text.

Contrary to Statement Analysis or SCAN which evaluates statements as either true or false, this approach differs in that they evaluate separately, portions of the statement as true or deceptive based on the density of cues in that portion. They selected 12 linguistic indicators of deception cited in the psychological and criminal justice literature that can be formally used to make these determinations. The indicators fall into three classes.

(1) Lack of commitment to a statement or declaration. The speaker uses linguistic devices to avoid making a direct statement of fact. Five of the indicators fit into this class:

> (i) Linguistic hedges (described below) including non-specific verbs, *I think* or *I believe*;

(ii) Qualified assertions, which leave open whether an act was performed, e.g. *I needed to get a weapon:*; *I thought about the gun in my dresser drawer*
(iii) Unexplained lapses of time, e.g. *later that day*;
(iv) Overzealous expressions, e.g. *I swear to God*
(v) Rationalization of an action, e.g. *I was unfamiliar with the road.*

(2) Preference for negative expressions in word choice, syntactic structure and semantics. This class comprises three indicators:

(i) Negative forms, either complete words such as *never* or negative morphemes as in *inconceivable*;
(ii) Negative emotions, e.g. *I was a nervous wreck*;
(iii) Memory loss, e.g. *I forget.*

(3) Inconsistencies with respect to verb and noun forms. Four of the indicators make up this class:

(i) Verb tense changes in which within a single frame of time, the tense of the verbs keep changing from present to past tense (described below);
(ii) Thematic role changes, e.g. changing the thematic role of a person from agent in one sentence to patient in another;
(iii) Noun phrase changes, where different name forms are used for the same referent or to change the focus of a narrative;
(iv)Pronoun changes (described below) which are similar to noun phrase changes. To clarify our explanation, three of the indicators are described in more detail below. It is important to note with respect to these indicators of deception that deceptive passages vary considerably in the types and mix of indicators used, and the particular words used within an indicator

type vary depending on factors such as race, gender, and socioeconomic status.

In terms of verb tense, past tense narrative is the norm for truthful accounts of past events according to most studies. However, the deviations from the past tense are the correlations with deception. Changes in verb tense are often more indicative of deception rather than the overall choice of tense. People may talk in a certain tense that may or may not be considered correct, yet it is the changes of this tense that require our attention. The most often cited example of tense change in a criminal statement is that of Susan Smith, who released the brake on her car letting her two small children inside plunge to their deaths. "I just feel hopeless," she said. "I can't do enough. My children wanted me. They needed me. And now I can't help them. I just feel like such a failure." While her statements about herself were presented in the present tense, those about her children were already in the past.

The terms 'hedge' and 'hedging' were introduced by George Lakoff to describe words "whose meaning implicitly involves fuzziness," e.g., *maybe, I guess,* and *sort of*. The use of hedges has been widely studied and correlated with deception. Hedge types include non-factual or specific verbs like *think* and *believe,* non-factual noun phrases like *my understanding* and *my recollection,* adjectives and adverbs like *possible* and *approximately*, indefinite noun phrases like *something* and *stuff*, and miscellaneous phrases like *a glimpse* and *between 9 and 9:30*. The hedge itself is affected by the person and the crime. The 285 hedges in Jeffrey Skilling's 7562 word Enron testimony include 21 cases of *my recollection*, 9 of *my understanding*, and 7 of *to my knowledge* while the 42 hedges in the car thief's 2282 word testimony include 6 cases of *shit* (*doing a little painting, and roofing, and shit*), 6 of *just* and 4 of *probably*. Despite the differences in style, the deceptive behavior in both cases is the same. Their educational, economic and social upbringing creates the difference hedging styles, yet they are the same for our purposes.

Hedging shows a lack of commitment. The following is a transcript of an oral statement of a college student who reported that a man broke into her apartment at 3:30 a.m. and raped her. A statement regarding such a traumatic experience should be filled with conviction, which this statement lacks.

"He grabbed me and held a knife to my throat. And when I woke up and I was, I mean I was really asleep and I didn't know what was going on, and I kind of you know I was scared and I kind of startled when I woke up, You know, You know I was startled and he, he told, he kept telling me to shut up and he asked me if I could feel the knife."

Consider the phrase, "I kind of startled when I woke up." This is not a normal reaction for a woman who awakens in the middle of the night to see an unknown man at her bed and to feel a knife at her throat. "Terrified" would seem to be more appropriate. Using the words "kind of startled" shows a change from the expected normal reaction of terror.

Studies of deception have found that deceivers tend to use fewer self-referencing expressions such as *I, my,* and *mine* than truth-tellers and fewer references to others. In the real world, it is difficult at best to determine a person's referential expression baseline. Therefore it is much easier to examine changes in these expressions. Like verb tense, changes in referential expressions can also be indicative of deception. Such changes in reference often involve the distancing of an item; for example, in the narrative of Captain McDonald, he describes 'my wife' and 'my daughter' sleeping, but he reports the crime to an emergency number as follows, with his wife and daughter referred to as *some people*:

So I told him that I needed a doctor and an ambulance and that some people had been stabbed.

149

Deceptive statements may also omit references entirely. Scott Peterson's initial police interview is characterized by a high number of omitted first person references:

> BROCCHINI: You drive straight home?
> PETERSON: To the warehouse, dropped off the boat.

The way we will want to utilize this information is to have the information for examination in written form. We will then choose one area of deception indication and mark all of the occurrences. An example of this would be to select the indication of "Hedges" and mark within the statement all of the listed hedges of "I believe" or "I think" "my recollection," etc. Then we can select another area of deception indication for example verb tense changes or overzealous statements.

Our goal is to provide a method of evaluating statements within a portion of an account. The subject may be telling the truth about basic issues while lying about specifics. In addition, rarely does anyone tell the entire truth about any topic. To save time, even when telling the truth, they will edit the story to fit their needs. This method helps you to identify the areas in the statement that may need to be readdressed.

Assessment Criteria Indicative of Deception (ACID)

Assessment Criteria Indicative of Deception or ACID combines content criteria derived from research in deception and memory along with investigative interviewing to facilitate the detection of deception. Research has found that fictional responses are shorter and have less supporting detail than true responses. This is because a lie is more cognitively demanding than telling the truth and liars must work harder to control their speech

Focus for ACID is placed on two (2) Criteria-Based Content Analysis or CBCA criteria from the Statement Valid Analysis or SVA interviewing process. These criteria are the Unstructured Production (Spontaneous Reproduction) and Quantity of Details (or Sufficient Detail). Like CBCA, Reality Monitoring (RM) decisions often are made from the amount and type of details in a statement. Memories for genuine events should contain more external-sensory details (color, smell, taste, etc.) and more contextual details. Examples:

External details – info gained from the senses. A **tall man** with **black hair** has 2 external details

Contextual details – the relationship between the details. The drugs were **on top** of the bed. I am sure about **the time** because I was **watching Jeopardy** which starts **every night at 7:00pm**.

Internal details – moods and experiences. I saw the man approach and **he frightened** me.

It is understood that a common strategy for deception is to prepare and practice a fictitious account or a "script lie." Therefore, the goal of the investigator is to increase the cognitive load making it difficult for the liar to deceive. They are unable to make changes to their prepared script without making the deception obvious. They will follow their lie script while a truthful subject relives the events.

151

The ACID system analyzes the length of responses, including potential errors and the details that were not provided during free recall, but were added in the course of later recall tasks. The process adds detail, requires multiple recall tasks, and includes alternative suggestions to the process which helps the honest person, but becomes nearly impossible for a deceptive subject to stay on script. This system, a combination of the others discussed, is processed in 8 steps.

1. Baseline and rapport – Not Scored
    a. 'Last meal'
    b. 'First day of work'
2. Free Recall 'Please describe detail, everything that happened.
    a. Free recall
3. Mental reinstatement of context 'Think about and include all sights, sounds, smells, emotions, thoughts, or anything else from time of event.'
    a. Mnemonics (memory aid)
4. Inferential block – Not Scored. This is a question asked so as to take their mind off immediate events.
    a. 'If your spouse had been present, would they have noticed something wrong?'
    b. 'Has a crime been committed?'
    c. 'Did anyone speak about anything illegal?'
5. Recall from other perspective
    a. 'If someone else had been in the room, what would they have seen?' –mnemonics
6. Reverse order recall 'Beginning with last, and ending with first, please describe the entire event in reverse order.'
    a. mnemonics
7. Inferential block 2
    a. 'Did you notice anything unusual about …….?'

b. 'Would anyone think that you did something you weren't supposed to ....?'

c. 'Do you think that you could have been mistaken about anything you have said so far?'

8. Retell entire event

a. 'Please describe, in as much detail as possible, everything that happened to make sure I have the entire story.

We are watching for issues like; the response length and the number of external, contextual, and internal details reported during free recall. Also the response length and the number of new external, contextual, and internal details reported during the mnemonic section of the interview. Lastly, whether or not the participant admitted that they could have made a mistake.

The mnemonic section of the process or memory aid is used to try and stimulate more information from the subject. The mnemonic section of honest statements consistently contain more details and are longer than the mnemonic section of deceptive statements because it enhances recall. Liars try to stay on script so the memory aid does not assist them because it is not part of the prepared recall. Also, honest people were more likely than deceivers to admit possible error. As we have seen, a liar believes that in order for you to believe their lie, the deception has to be accepted in whole. No part can be false. The free recall portion became a baseline as truth tellers expanded later in mnemonics while liars told the same amount of information. This is similar to measuring the statement for balance as we did with SCAN except now we are balancing the recall with the mnemonic section of the statement.

It all makes sense when you exam the process naturally. You recall events, but we simply are not able to tell a step by step detailed illustration of the event. Our mind will remember yet our ability to write and/or think is substantially slower. Therefore our mind will process the information and explain what it thinks is important. This is true only for the truth tellers. The deceivers have to work their way through what they want to tell you and will generally lock in on a particular script. It is this script which will eventually lead to their demise. If after someone tells all that there is to tell on a subject and then you ask them several mnemonic questions, it should cause them to recall more information and in the context of the last recall, add it to their explanation. This in turn will cause this section of the story to be longer than the first free recall. Script regurgitations are simply that, word vomit. They are unable to add or shorten the context of the story to stay on script.

Handwriting Analysis

I wanted to include this short and simple examination at what some consider important and others compare to a circus act. Either way, I find the thought processes behind the idea intriguing. Though not overly effective, you will find much of the material factual. Handwriting analysis adds value because it can show in some instances the type of person involved in the writing along with their cognitive loads and personalities. Everyone has different handwriting because we all have different structural designs of the hands, fingers, etc. Handwriting is considered by many as the brain writing. Our conscious decides what we will write, but the subconscious determines how we will write. Extroverts tend to write with large letters, while introverts with small letters. A much focused mind that seeks perfection will also write very deliberate and small. A good example of focused mind writing is Albert Einstein. His letter expression is small and almost perfect.

The lower case "t" can tell you about how a person feels. This letter has two parts, the vertical line or stem and the horizontal line or T-bar. When a person writes, look for the placement of the T-bar on the stem. The higher the T-bar on the stem, the higher the person's self-esteem while below half way of the stem can indicate they are afraid of failure or lack confidence.

The letter "i" is the same as the "t" except we are looking at the placement of the dot. To the left of the stem, they may procrastinate, while to the right of the stem shows they are driven. The dot placed directly above the stem shows they are careful, or too high above the stem could mean they are unrealistic. If they replace the dot with a circle or happy face, this person may be immature.

The letter "o" is believed to say a lot about a person's feelings. A loop to the left inside the circle shows self-denial; a loop to the right may be deception. A double looped "o" or an "o" that has two (2) loops inside the circle indicates caution because it shows the writer

155

retracing a letter or placing excessive pressure. The boldness of the letter will stand out signifying that this is at a point of the statement which is causing cognitive load. The brain is trying to work out what to write while the hand sits and waits for the decision, but is unable to sit idle.

The Felons Claw involves the letters g, y, and z. This is an action of placing a sickle or hook at the lower end of the letter. About 80% of the prison population acquires this style, hence its name. The person who utilizes this writing trait is said to be self-destructive.

It is a fun topic and everyone should explore its foundations thoroughly. The more we understand about writing and sentence structure the more effective investigator you will become. These small inferences can assist you in determining the mindset of the interviewee. As we learned earlier, personality observations are critical to the required interview style.

Common Errors by Lie Detectors

12

Once you eliminate the impossible, whatever remains, no matter how improbable, must be the truth.
                    - Sherlock Holmes by Sir Arthur Conan Doyle

Examining the wrong cues

Despite being common examples, gaze aversion and grooming are not reliable indicators of deception. Only a decrease of illustrators has been recognized as a reliable singular observation to deceptive behaviors. Many observers who were led to believe someone was lying overestimated nonverbal cues and sought out information to confirm their bias. They will also downplay information to prove the innocence of the suspects.

Overemphasis on nonverbal cues

Dependent on the circumstances, too much attention can be applied to nonverbal cues because we are accustomed to people watching. The nonverbal cues observed can cause a predetermination of guilt for the viewers. Don't judge a book by its cover. It takes time and effort to formulate and ask the best questions.

An example of this over-emphasis in non-verbal behaviors occurred in Chapter 5, the fifth Fatal Error was

Recognizing Danger. In addition, one of the deceptive traits of murdered officers also from Chapter 5 is; Feels they can "read" others/situations and will drop guard as a result.

Speech content is more accurate than nonverbal cues

There are a number of explanations that lead us to place too much information on the verbal cues and not enough on the verbal indications. These are some of the most common:

- The Othello Effect - We must always remember that a truth teller can be as nervous as a liar out of fear of being wrongly accused or fear of us thinking of them as liars. These behaviors will lead us to say someone is guilty by their nonverbal characteristics alone without taking into account all of the other circumstances or evidence.
- Heuristics - These are general decision rules. The overall population believes everyone is innocent causing them to make insufficient decisions while cops feel the opposite causing guilt biased decisions. The letter of the law is that everyone is innocent until proven guilty. We all know that this can sometimes be reversed.
- Neglect of interpersonal differences - The tendency to interpret nervous behaviors as suspicious without taking individual differences into account. An example would be the social clumsiness of introverts and the impression created of tension, nervousness, or fear that is naturally given off by socially anxious individuals.
- Neglect of intrapersonal variations - This happens in the rapport stage. Engaging in small talk and discussing the crime itself are fundamentally different situations. Small talk is low stress while talk of the crime is high stress. The observable behaviors and responses have to be in the

company of stress. Without it, no one has the fear of lying.

- Existing Interview Techniques - Law enforcement are sometimes advised to confront suspects at the beginning of the interview with the evidence they have. Disclosing evidence early provides liars with the opportunity to change their stories and provides an innocent explanation for the evidence. Be careful about accusing someone of lying because it can cause them to shut down (Why talk you're not going to believe me anyways).
- Overconfidence in lie detecting skills - Many in our profession are overconfident in their abilities in believing they can catch a liar. Again it falls to us to enter the scenario and try to not only show proof of the person's guilt but to equally try and show their innocence. Our truth finding efforts will pay off as long as we have placed the necessary efforts and examined all of the evidence.

Avoiding the Errors

We must pay attention to both verbal and nonverbal cues. Police often refuse to believe much of the information presented because it may contradict what they consider occurred. Avoid relying only on nonverbal cues alone. Countless studies showed that in order to detect lies, listening carefully to what is said is necessary and paying attention only to behavior impairs lie detection.

The best classifications of truths and lies are made when both sets of cues are taken into account. There are three (3) ways to help you pay attention to both verbal and nonverbal cues:

- We can take into account both nonverbal and verbal cues without looking at the relation between the two sets of cues. In other words, examine each set of cues in their single context. What are the verbal cues saying and then what are the nonverbal cues demonstrating.

- Examine nonverbal behavior in relation to speech content watching for any mismatches between the two. Are their nonverbal cues matching what would be expected of their verbal cues? At a point of the narrative, the subject is telling a very excited portion of the events, yet their nonverbal show a lack of illustrators.
- Avoid the Othello effect of misidentifying signs of nervousness. Establish a specific baseline of behavior and personality type of the subject to help you determine their nervous behavior as simply normal or indicative of deceit.

There are two (2) interview styles; informational-gathering and accusatory. We must try to stay with the informational-gathering style to keep them talking. Accusatorial questions can cause them to shut down. The longer they talk the longer you have to catch them in a lie and the informational-gathering style also projects less stress to help prevent a false confession.

Exploit the different psychological states of truth tellers and liars via two different approaches; Strategic questioning and cognitive loading. Either way requires the person to talk. Ask unanticipated questions to break a lie script through cognitive loading.

"Where were you between 4-5pm?"
"I was at the gym."
"How many others were there?"
"Who was working the desk?"
"Who else saw you there?"

These are questions which could cause the subject to fall out of the prepared script because they are areas which they may not have considered during their script prep.

Compared with liars, truth tellers should be able to recall the event through various approaches to the story.

"How old are you?" followed by the question, "what is your date of birth?" is more difficult to answer for liars resulting in longer delays than for truth tellers.

Lying is already difficult but by loading more thought processes, it becomes harder. One way is the reverse order retell of the events and the other is having them maintain eye contact with you at all times during the explanation. This adds stress because when people have to concentrate, they are inclined to look away occasionally to a motionless point. Maintaining eye contact is distracting. A truth teller will still be able to express the recall truths but a liar will have a difficult time.

Specific or strategic questions or the Devil's Advocate's questioning approach. This line of questioning can be important in many security settings like border security or risk assessments of informants. They are asked for their opinion for and against their specific area of information. ("What are your reasons for supporting the Americans in the war in Afghanistan?" vs. Playing devil's advocate, "Is there anything you can say against the involvement of the Americans in Afghanistan?")

People normally think more deeply about and are able to generate reasons that support rather than oppose their beliefs and opinions. Truth tellers are likely to provide more information in their responses to the opinion-eliciting question than to the devil's advocate question. Truth tellers' answers are longer than their devil's advocate answers. Also, the truth tellers' answers sounded more direct and believable while revealing more emotional involvement than did their devil's advocate answers.

This line of questioning could have been used December 30, 2009 in Afghanistan. The CIA had used a polygraph to determine the truthful intentions of an informant who wanted to give them information on Taliban and Al Qaeda members. They were aware of his extremist views against the Americans but decided after the polygraph that he was using it as a cover. The subject was brought to a CIA building where he blew himself up killing 7 CIA agents.

The strategic use of evidence: Guilty suspects are inclined to use avoidance strategies or denial strategies. A man has his wallet stolen from his office drawer. You have fingerprints that indicate who opened the drawer but you do not disclose this to the suspect. Have them describe their activities in the office. They will deny being around the drawer. Then you can ask questions about the area where the wallet had been and see how they respond. Again the subject has denial of any knowledge. The final phase is to reveal the fingerprints and ask them to explain the contradictions.

Preventing False Confessions

A false confession is an admission of guilt in a crime in which the confessor is not responsible for the crime. Even though false confessions might appear to be the exception, they occur on a regular basis and false confessions are becoming a greater reality. Care has to be taken by the investigator to ensure the validity of the confession. Many of us believe that no one would confess to a crime they had not committed. Yet it is believed that about 5% of confessions could be false based on 25% of the DNA overturned cases.

According to a study out of Northwestern University, in Illinois, of 55 wrongfully convicted defendants who confessed or the conviction was based upon a codefendants confession:

83.6% police misconduct
27.3% prosecutorial misconduct
25.5% false or misleading forensic evidence
30.9% incorrect eyewitness testimony
70.9% testimony by informants

Adult false confessions occur when:

- Evidence is so stacked against the subject; they begin to believe that they are the only one who could have committed the crime.
- They become exhausted after extremely long interrogations.
- Authorities misconstrue suspect's innocent statements as guilty admissions.
- Suspects are duped into believing all will be alright by admitting to the crime.

Presumptions during the interview can lead to "bias" or tunnel vision. This can lead to a condition known as confirmation bias which is only the information that gives credence to your expectations are valid and all other information is discounted.

It has been found that offers of leniency and minimization tactics showed an increase in guilty confessions of 72% over false confessions of 20%. This verifies the practice of offering leniency in exchange for a confession. Juveniles and mentally impaired subjects are the most vulnerable to a false confession and require extreme caution when being interviewed.

Statement Validity Analysis was developed for and is showing great promise in interviewing these groups. Most proven false confessions occur with murder and rape cases. The primary causes are:

- Overly long interrogations
- Presentations of false evidence
- Investigator tunnel vision
- Prolonged isolation
- Lack of sleep

One corrective measure is to videotape the entire process. Once the video process begins, do not allow any other interviews to occur once the taping has stopped. This not only protects the accused but also protects your agency from any accusations of abuse. Our normal process is to develop theories and prove them correct. It is equally important to try and disprove them.

- Have another investigator view the interview process.
- Independently verify the information given is case specific and not gathered from officer's statements and media.
- Verify the evidence to the statements provided.

Assassinations and Serial Killings

13

Come as you are. Bring what cha got.

Comment from a U.S. Special Forces Operator when asked about sending in SOF to try and rescue our personnel from the Benghazi, Libya U.S. Embassy attack where 4 Americans were killed and help never arrived.

Exceptional Case Study Project (ECSP)

The ECSP is a joint study by the United States Secret Service (USSS) and several psychiatrists in an effort to determine if there are patterns to an attacker or if a line of questioning could be developed to separate legitimate threats from hoaxes. From 1949 to 1996, it was discovered that 83 subjects participated in 73 incidents and were identified and known to have attacked or came close to an attacking a prominent public official or figure just in the United States. There were a variety of motives listed in the study that included: notoriety, revenge, idiosyncratic thinking, hopes to be killed, interest in bringing about political change, and money. Idiosyncratic beliefs, like a wish to save the world, bring attention to a perceived wrong, or desire for a special relationship with the target, filled 40% of the incidents. These subjects were found to be more likely to attack a public figure like a celebrity than a protected official. Subjects with motives like notoriety or a wish to be killed by law enforcement were more likely to attack the President. These subjects were at the time of the incident:

Ages 16-73
Half received at least some college
Near lethal attackers were likely to be single and never married rather than attackers

Study Results
- Women were more likely to be attackers rather than approachers. Subjects who targeted the President were more likely to be full-time employed. Both had a history of transience.
- Most were social isolates, but one third was not.
- Many had a history of harassing other persons.
- Most had a history of explosive, angry behavior and half had a history of violent behavior.
- Few had histories of arrest for violent crimes or weapons.
- Few had ever been incarcerated.
- Most had a history of weapons use but no formal training.
- Most had an interest in militant ideas and groups but were not active members of any.
- Many had a history of depression.
- Many were known to have attempted suicide.
- Many had had contact with a Mental Health Facility but did not reveal their considerations.
- Attackers were less likely to have delusional ideas or be delusional than were near lethal approachers.
- Few had histories of command hallucinations.
- Few had a history of substance abuse.

- Almost all American assassins, attackers, or would-be attackers believed they had difficulties coping with problems in their life.
- All, at some point, came to see an attack as a solution for their problems.
- Fewer than a quarter of the subjects are known to have developed an escape plan.
- One third of the subjects expected to be killed.
- None lived an exemplary life and had difficulties maintaining a consistent relationship, job performance and achievements.
- Not "losers," half college, two fifths had been married, one third were parents, completed military service, one attended law school, another medical school, another was a retired police officer, another a firefighter, postal worker, and several engineers.
- One truth was that the events began after a period of downward spiral in their lives in the 12 months prior to the event.
- Most are preventable because always follow a path to the attack.
- There may be interest in previous attacks.
- They are likely to communicate their intentions to others or keep a journal.
- This is also true for stalkers and certain types of workplace violence.
- Very few made threats to their targets or police.
- If a threat is made it should be taken serious because the lack of concern can be perceived as permission to proceed.
- They will practice and carry out visits to the targets office, home, or visiting places.
- They will often choose several targets choosing the target after knowing the opportunity exist and it will fulfill their goals.
- Few have much cunning and lack the bravado that many perceive them as having.

"Threat assessment" is the term used to describe the set of investigative and operational techniques that can be used by law enforcement professionals to identify, assess, and manage the risks of targeted violence and its potential perpetrators. Violence is a process, as well as an act. Careful analysis of violent incidents shows that violent acts often are the culmination of long-developing, identifiable trails of problems, conflicts, disputes, and failures. A key to investigation and resolution of threat assessment cases is identification of the subject's "attack-related" behaviors. Violence is the product of an interaction among three factors:

a) The individual who takes violent action.
b) Stimulus or triggering conditions that lead the subject to see violence as an option, "way out," or solution to problems or life situation.
c) A setting that facilitates or permits the violence, or at least does not stop it from occurring.

Perpetrators of targeted acts of violence engage in discrete behaviors that precede and are linked to their attacks; they consider, plan, and prepare before engaging. The threat assessment approach is a fact-based method of evaluation developed by the USSS. Although it was developed based on data used to attack or attempt to attack public officials, with modification it can be used to evaluate other forms of targeted violence. This approach is innovative in two ways:
(1) it does not rely on descriptive, demographic, or psychological profiles and (2) it does not rely on verbal or written threats as a threshold for risk. It moves away from classic profiles and looks at ideas and behaviors that may lead to violent behavior.
Profiles are useful for eliminating the field of suspects after the crime. Instead of looking at demographic and psychological characteristics, the threat assessment approach focuses on a subject's thinking and behaviors. The question is not what does the person look like, but has the subject engaged in recent behavior

that suggests that they are moving on a path toward violence. Investigators make a distinction between people who make threats and those who pose a threat.

Persons who appear to pose a threat provoke the greatest level of concern. Very few of these threateners have ever made an attempt to harm someone. None of the people who attacked a public figure in the last 50 years ever directly communicated the threat. Attack-related behaviors may move along a continuum. Preparatory behaviors including selection and location of the target, securing a weapon, subverting security measures, etc. Behaviors of concern include:

(1) An unusual interest in instances of targeted violence
(2) Evidence of ideas or plans to attack a specific target (e.g., diary notes, recent acquisition of a weapon),
(3) Communications of inappropriate interest or plans to attack a target to family, friends, co-workers, etc.
(4) Following a target or visiting a possible location of an attack
(5) Approaching a target or protected setting

The U.S. Secret Service, based on experience and assassination research, has identified 10 key questions to guide a protective intelligence or threat assessment investigation:

1: What motivated the subject to make the statements, or take the action, that caused him/her to come to attention?
2: What has the subject communicated to anyone concerning his/her intentions?
3: Has the subject shown an interest in targeted violence, perpetrators of targeted violence, weapons, extremist groups, or murder?

4: Has the subject engaged in attack-related behavior, including any menacing, harassing, and/or stalking-type behavior?

5: Does the subject have a history of mental illness involving command hallucinations, delusional ideas, feelings of persecution, etc. with indications that the subject has acted on those beliefs?

6: How organized is the subject? Is he/she capable of developing and carry out a plan?

7: Has the subject experienced a recent loss and or loss of status, and has this led to feelings of desperation and despair?

8: Corroboration - What is the subject saying and is it consistent with his/her actions?

9: Is there concern among those that know the subject that he/she might take action based on inappropriate ideas?

10: What factors in the subject's life and/or environment might increase/decrease the likelihood of the subject attempting to attack a target?

These threat assessments can also be utilized in common stalker cases. Collecting intelligence and gathering information from sources can enhance your interdiction of this person from carrying out the threats. If someone is contemplating these actions, the more matches that they possess within this threat assessment, the greater the likelihood the threat is credible.

Serial Killings

There are many, both in law enforcement and academia, who study serial killers extensively. I wanted to include serial killers because they are examined, profiled and identified based on behaviors. A serial killer is separated in category from spree killers and mass killers by their actions as demonstrated by the chart below.

	Mass	Spree	Serial
# victims	4+	2+	2+
# events	1	1	2+
# locations	1	2+	2+
Cooling-off	no	no	yes

Note: The number of victims for serial killers was revised from 3 to 2 at the 2005 by the FBI.

As shown, a serial killer must have 2 or more killings from 2 or more separate events which occur in different locations and have a cooling off period or a time frame that they stop killing. 88% of all serial killers will be male and average 29 years of age at the time of their first killing.

A Modus Operandi or MO is the actions taken by the offender to perpetrate the offense. It relates to the degree of criminal sophistication on the part of the offender. The MO is a learned behavior that evolves as the offender becomes more sophisticated and confident. It may change or be improved upon as he gains in experience, learning from previous mistakes relating to issues of the crime. Change can also occur for the protection of the offender's identity as well as their escape from the scene.

In a serial killers pattern of behavior can exist a signature. It is related to the motivation of the offender and is a significant pattern of behavior that is personal to the offender to conduct in the scene.

A third event, commonly espoused in the public's mind as common is staging. Staging occurs when someone purposely alters the scene prior to the arrival of the police. It is normally performed to direct the investigation away from the suspect, be a part of a ritual, or add to the shock value.

We have all heard of MO, signatures and staging with respect to a serial killer, but they are not the norm. A MO will change as will the events of a crime. The killer will learn from experience and try to make adjustments in the next incident to correct issues they did not like in the previous event. Therefore, with an ever changing set of rules, the MO also changes. A signature to a crime scene is actually a rarity. It makes for exciting writing and story lines, yet is not as common as the public believes. A signature is actually a subset of a ritual behavior. A study by the Journal of the American Academy of Psychiatry and the Law was conducted in 2010 of 38 sexually motivated serial homicide offenders and their 162 victims involving cases supplied by the FBI's Behavioral Science Unit. The average number of murders committed by the offenders was 4.2.

A ritual was defined as crime scene acts by the offenders that were "unnecessary for the perpetration of the homicide, involved activity that exceeded that which could cause death, and occurred with at least two victims. Examples include body posing, foreign object insertions, torture, or overkill that occurred with two or more victims in a series."

A signature was defined as a ritualistic act that was a distinct or unique behavior, not seen at any other crime scene (e.g., eye removal); a ritualistic act that was a unique or distinctive way to carry out a familiar act (e.g., posing victims, but with legs spread and propped up on pillows); or a combination of acts that, when taken together, were distinctive and unique (e.g., inserting vegetables into victims and photographing them).

There were thirty-seven (97.4%) of the 38 offenders engaged in ritualistic behaviors with at least two victims in their homicide series. Of the 162 homicides

172

studied, 147 (90.7%) involved ritualistic acts. Of the 37 offenders who engaged in some type of ritualistic behavior, 33 (89.2%) did so with all their victims. Of the four offenders who did not engage in ritualistic behavior at every crime scene, one engaged in ritualistic behavior with 29 percent of his victims, one with 40 percent, one with 60 percent, and one with 80 percent.

The most common ritualistic acts were:

Act	No	%
Penis penetration	20	39.2
Binding	18	31.6
Overkill	17	25.3
Beating	11	21.5
Posing	13	17.7
Mutilation	10	13.3
Trophies and souvenirs	6	12.0
Photographs and documentation	4	11.4
Dismemberment	5	9.5
Foreign object insertion	9	8.9
Torture	4	7.6
Biting	4	7.0
Gagging	7	6.3
Necrophilia	3	1.9

Of the 37 offenders who engaged in ritualistic behavior, only 5 (13.5%) used exactly the same ritual with every victim in the series. 31 (83.8%) of the 37 offenders engaged in ritual behaviors which were behaviorally similar with at least two of their victims. However, an offender engaged in recognizable and repetitive signature behaviors in only 18 percent of his homicides.

The notion that offenders leave unique signatures at every scene is not supported by any data. Although most of the offenders engaged in some form of ritualistic behavior, they rarely engaged in exactly the same behavior at every murder.

Almost half of the subjects experimented at one or sometimes more crime scenes which created unique behaviors to that scene. This type of crime scene behavior could easily lead an investigator who is inexperienced with serial sexual murder cases to conclude incorrectly that such different behavior indicates the work of another offender.

Contrary to popular belief, only two offenders evidenced any type of psychosis, and in both cases, the offender's psychotic symptoms were not at all connected to any of their homicides or to their ritualistic or signature behaviors. Most events were the result of carrying out fantasies.

Another important fact to understand is that serial killers are perceived to be of higher intellect. The fact is the opposite. Rarely do we see, even the notorious Ted Bundy, someone who exhibits above average intellect. Most are not caught because of their intellect; in fact most are caught by the idiotic mistakes they make. It is also important to recognize that these profiles can carry over to arson and rape investigations

What is some of the information that can be obtained with a criminal profile? With a properly trained and experienced investigator with a good eye for the crime scene, assisted by careful crime scene technicians, we may be able to deduct some of the following:

Age
Sex
Race
Marital Status
Intelligence Scholastic Achievement
Life-Style
Rearing Environment
Social Adjustment
Personality Style/Characteristics
Appearance/grooming
Residence in relation to Crime Scene
Vehicle
Socio-economic Status
Sexual Adjustment
Type of Sexual perversion

Prior Criminal Record
Motive

There are two types of crime scene, Organized and Disorganized. Some differences between the two include but are not limited to:

Disorganized Offenders:
- behavior is unpredictable
- lacks criminal sophistication
- all ages
- different races
- alcohol or drug use
- prior institutionalization
- futile attempt to disguise handwriting
- lower to middle class
- poor communication skills
- unemployed, sloppy
- older car, if at all

Organized Offenders:
- average intelligence
- criminal sophistication
- criminal history may include financial or property crimes
- good communication skills
- middle class
- sporadic employment
- neat appearance/well-maintained vehicle
- owns a well maintained late model vehicle

Any one crime may reveal characteristics of both the organized and disorganized personalities. A crime may transform from organized to disorganized, however the reverse is rare. A shift from organized to disorganized can occur as a result of drug or alcohol use, lack of criminal experience, or the youth of the offender.
In domestic homicides, where a family member kills another family member, one or several cues can be

indicative. The victim, usually the female, will rarely be found nude. Though he killed her, she is still his wife and he does not want others to view her nude. If suicide is suspected, the suicide note will be typed. This occurred post mortem and the suspect knows they will not be able to duplicate the handwriting. Another sign of domestic homicide is the deceased spouse was the least threat to an intruder. Often times the killer will try to cover the events of the crime with the excuse that someone broke into the home and murdered their wife. An armed intruder will usually have the most to fear from the husband. If a threat is to be eliminated, they will not kill the least threat (wife) and leave the husband. Another determination of domestic homicide is by interviewing neighbors, friends and family to determine if the deceased was scared of their significant other. Violence will follow a path and has a tendency to escalate.

There is much more involved in this topic though I have left much out to prevent someone from possibly making adjustments to their activities to avoid detection. It is still an area which requires a lot more study and more investigators should be trained in the techniques. Not so they can become mind readers, but to help them in thoroughly exploring homicide, rape and arson scenes.

Below is a list of serial killings by decade. As with much in society, changes are occurring with serial killers as well.

Decade	White	Black	Hispanic	Asian	Native
1900	62.5	37.5	0.0	0.0	0.0
1910	45.7	54.3	0.0	0.0	0.0
1920	72.4	27.6	0.0	0.0	0.0
1930	53.6	46.4	0.0	0.0	0.0
1940	63.0	29.6	3.7	0.0	3.7
1950	79.5	20.5	0.0	0.0	0.0
1960	68.7	29.8	0.0	0.0	1.5
1970	62.0	33.6	3.3	0.6	0.6
1980	54.3	37.0	6.6	0.6	1.5
1990	41.8	52.3	4.6	1.3	0.0
2000	28.4	68.6	1.5	1.0	0.5
2010	12.5	75.0	12.5	0.0	0.0
TOTAL	52.0	42.8	3.8	0.7	0.8

The End of the Shift

14

If you are familiar with my books, then you already know they always end with a chapter called, "The End of The Shift." This is the time each day either after your shift has concluded or your career has comes to an end. It is the most important day for the rest of your life. I have discussed the issues of our divorce rates, suicide rates and alcohol abuse. Stress has been explored as the root cause of most of our physical and mental ailments. It is a profession of confrontation that can rarely last more than a few decades. It is in the street where conflict occurs and it is through confrontation that most of our greatest stressors originate.

I am going to keep this section much shorter than the other books where I explained each of these concepts in detail. Society is at war with itself. America is embroiled in a war, not in the Middle East, but here on our streets. As law enforcement officers, you are the front line troops. The difference is in how the war is fought. There are few winners and many losers. The best we can achieve is the maintenance of basic order. There will always be bad guys and a need for police officers. The differences are occurring in the upcoming generations whose belief systems are being formed by a media and leaders who continue to meld distorted ideas of truths and freedoms.

With all that troubles our society today, I watch in amazement the topics that have become critical to the sheep of society like drug legalization and gun control. It is an interesting dichotomy of people and their generations who actually believe these are the pressing topics of the day. The one that bothers me the most is the belief that drug legalization will make any positive changes to our country or society. It is just as sad that the majority, who could stand up and say "enough is enough" and put an end to all of these ridiculous topics, choose to sit idle. Yet as we have seen over and over, the mainstream fails to stand up for itself and avoids that great stressor; confrontation. As Col. David Grossman likes to put it, there are the sheep, the wolves and the sheepdogs. The sheep make up for about 98% of the total population while the other 2% is equally divided between the sheepdogs and the wolves. The sheep do not like the sheepdogs, but they have a clear understanding that when the wolves are around, the sheep want the sheepdogs close by. The sheep ultimately become victims twice; once when they are attacked by the wolves and again while living in the constant fear of another attack.

If you have decided upon a career in law enforcement, you must learn to deal with confrontation from both the sheep and the wolves. There will be a strain that begins to wear you down over time. Stand true to your principles which brought you here to begin with and help teach others how to stand again. Only collectively shall we ever become the majority that we have always been.

Acknowledgements

To initiate this page means that another book has finished. This is my third book in a "Trilogy" of officer safety issues. I have many people to thank for their time and patience in allowing me to pick their brain for this project. The very first I need to thank are the readers themselves. Most are the professionals who keep our society safe from evil. Everywhere I have lectured has been a delight and the feedback on the books, fantastic. Thank You All!

My thanks also to Jorge Santamaria, my former partner, supervisor, friend and co-instructor who helped me in this endeavor by sharing his vast knowledge of polygraphy.

Thanks to my former patrol partner and current co-instructor Joe Morris who has listened to and provided ideas for many topics.

Thanks to all of my former partners from the Patrol, each retired and hopefully enjoying this ride as much as me.

A very special notation is required to my former partner, friend, and companion Draco, who never once let me down, cared about my moods, complained about the hours, watched over me in moments of danger, and comforted me in times of sadness; I am eternally grateful and miss you.

The biggest thanks of all has to be extended to my family who has each tolerated the career and now my obsession in writing; Toni, Steven, and Vanessa. Especially to my loving and caring wife Toni, who always allows me the time and space to accomplish my dreams; I love you.

Bibliography

Adams, Susan (April 2003). COMMUNICATION UNDER STRESS: INDICATORS OF VERACITY AND DECEPTION IN WRITTEN NARRATIVES.

Assessment of Optimal Interrogation Approaches.

Assessment Criteria Indicative of Deception (ACID): An Integrated System of Investigative Interviewing and Detecting Deception; KEVIN COLWELL, CHERYL K. HISCOCK-ANISMAN, AMINA MEMON, LAURA TAYLOR and JESSICA PREWETT; Journal of Investigative Psychology and Offender Profiling, J. Investig. Psych. Offender Profi l. 4: 167–180 (2007).

Blandon-Gitlin, Iris; Pezdek, Kathy; Lindsay, D. Stephen; Hagen, Lisa; Criteria-based Content Analysis of True and Suggested Accounts of Events; APPLIED COGNITIVE PSYCHOLOGY Appl. Cognit. Psychol. 23: 901–917 (2009) Published online 11 August 2008 in Wiley InterScience

Buckley, Wendy; Adult ESOL Instructor; November 2010; Overview of "What Every Body Is Saying by Joe Navarro, 2008.

Colwell, Kevin, Hiscock-Anisman, Memon, Amina, Taylor, Laura, Prewett, Jessica; Assessment Criteria Indicative of Deception (ACID): An Integrated System of Investigative Interviewing and Detecting Deception; Journal of Investigative Psychology and Offender Profiling

J. Investig. Psych. Offender Profi l. 4: 167–180 (2007)

Conducting Effective Interviews; AICPA Forensic and Valuation Services Section

Coram, Robert (2002). Boyd, The Fighter Pilot Who Changed the Art of War, Little, Brown and Company.

Criteria-based Content Analysis of True and Suggested Accounts of Events; IRIS BLANDO´ N-GITLIN, KATHY PEZDEK2, D. STEPHEN LINDSAY and LISA HAGEN; Published online 11 August 2008 in Wiley InterScience.

CRITERIA-BASED CONTENT ANALYSIS (CBCA) IN STATEMENT CREDIBILITY ASSESSMENT; Verónica Godoy-Cervera and Lorenzo Higueras, Papeles del Psicólogo, 2005. Vol. 26, pp. 92-98.

Detecting Deception; Dr. Mike Aamodt, Radford University, presentation

DOD Defense Academy for Credibility Assessment; Final Report May 2007,

DOD Polygraph Department, Seeking the Truth, June 1991

Ekman, Paul, Telling Lies, Berkley Books 1987.

False Confessions: Causes, Consequences, and Implications; Richard A. Leo, PhD, JD; The Journal of the American Academy of Psychiatry and the Law, 2009.

Fast, Julius (1973). The Body Language of Sex, Power, and Aggression. M Evans and Company Inc.

Final Report, May 2007, Assessment of Optimal Interrogation Approaches, MIPR#H9C101-G-0051. The Department of Defense, Defense Academy for Credibility Assessment

Givens, David G. 2009. The Nonverbal Dictionary of Gestures, Signs & Body Language Cues. Spokane: Center for Nonverbal Studies (http://www.center-for-nonverbal-studies.org/6101.html)

Horvath, E, Jayne, B., and Buckley, J., "Differentiation of Truthful and Deceptive Criminal Suspects in Behavior

Analysis Interviews,"Journal of Forensic Sciences, JFSCA, Vol. 39, No. 3, May 1994, pp. 793-807

H. Stefan Bracha, M.D., Tyler C. Ralston, M.A., Jennifer M. Matsukawa, M.A., National Center for PTSD, Department of Veterans Affairs, Pacific Islands Health Care System, Spark M. Matsunaga Medical Center, Honolulu, Hawaii, Andrew E. Williams, M.A., Department of Psychology, University of Hawaii at Manoa, Honolulu, Hawaii, and Adam S. Bracha, B.A., Biomedical-Research Consultant, Honolulu, Hawaii, Does "Fight or Flight" Need Updating?

Jaume Masip , Siegfried L. Sporer , Eugenio Garrido & Carmen Herrero (2005):
The detection of deception with the reality monitoring approach: a review of the empirical evidence, Psychology, Crime & Law, 11:1, 99-122

Knapp, M.L., Hart, R.P., and Dennis, H.S. 1974. An exploration of deception as a communication construct. Human Communication Research, 1, 15-29.

Lakoff, G. 1972. Hedges: A study in meaning criteria and the logic of fuzzy concepts. In 4 7 Papers from the 8th Regional Meeting, Chicago Linguistic Society

Learning To Listen, Facilitator Guide; Second Edition;by HRDQ

Leo, Richard A., False Confessions: Causes, Consequences, and Implications, J Am Acad Psychiatry Law 37:332–43, 2009

Lying Words: Predicting Deception From Linguistic Styles; Matthew L. Newman, James W. Pennebaker,; Diane S. Berry; Jane M. Richards

Madden, Timothy J, Sgt CSP (2006). Investigative Interview Techniques.

Matsumoto, David; Sung Hwang; Hyi; Skinner, Lisa; and Frank, Mark. Evaluating Truthfulness and Detecting Deception

McClish, Mark (2011). 10 Easy Ways To Spot A Liar: The best techniques of Statement Analysis, Nonverbal Communication and Handwriting Analysis.

Miller, Laurence, Personality-guided interview and interrogation, Practical psychology for law enforcement investigators

National Research Council. The Polygraph and Lie Detection . Washington, DC: The National Academies Press, 2003.

Navarro, Joe (2008). What Every BODY is Saying: An Ex-FBI Agent's Guide to Speed-Reading People, William Morrow Paperbacks

Newman, M. L., Pennebaker, J. W., Berry, D. S. and J. M. Richards. 2003. Lying words: predicting deception from linguistic styles. Personality and Social Psychology Bulletin. 29, 665-675.

Ost, James, Aldert Vrij, Alan Costall & Ray Bull. Crashing memories and reality monitoring: Distinguishing between perceptions, imaginations and 'false memories.' Department of Psychology, University of Portsmouth, Portsmouth, Hampshire.

Personality-guided interview and interrogation; Practical psychology for law enforcement investigators By Laurence Miller, PhD.

Pitfalls and Opportunities in Nonverbal and Verbal Lie Detection, Aldert Vrij, Pa¨r Anders Granhag, and Stephen Porter; Psychological Science in the Public Interest; 11(3) 89–121.

Porter, Wayne. Serial Killer presentation.

Protective Intelligence and Threat Assessment: A Guide for State and Local Law Enforcement Officials, by Robert A. Fein and Bryan Vossekuil, May 1998, USDOJ

Reading Between the Lies; Dr. Paul Ekman; September, October, November, December, 2009 Volume 2, number4.

Renaud, Ray, COMPARISON! COMPARISON! COMPARISON!

Ritual and Signature in Serial Sexual Homicide, Louis B. Schlesinger, PhD, Martin Kassen, MA, V. Blair Mesa, MA and Anthony J. Pinizzotto, PhD. J Am Acad Psychiatry Law 38:2:239-246 (June 2010), Copyright © 2013 by the American Academy of Psychiatry and the Law.

Sapir, A. 1987. *Scientific Content Analysis(SCAN)*. Laboratory of Scientific Interrogation. Phoenix, AZ.

Sapir, A. 1995. *The View Guidebook: Verbal Inquiry – the Effective Witness*. Laboratory of Scientific Interrogation. Phoenix, AZ.

Serial Killer Statistics; Aamodt, M. G. (2012, September 9). Serial killer statistics..

Serial Killers; Dr. Mike Aamodt, Radford University. Presentation.

Sheppard, Peter (March 2009). Transforming the Mind.

Statement Analysis Presentation, Patrick J Kelly.

Techniques and Controversies in the Interrogation of Suspects: The Artful Practice versus the Scientific Study; Allison D. Redlich, Christian Meissner; J. L. Skeem, K. Douglas, & S. Lilienfeld (Eds.), Psychological science in the courtroom: Controversies and consensus.

The FBI Law Enforcement Bulletin, March 2006, Volume 75 Number 3.

Varnell, Steven (2010). "Criminal Interdiction", Dog Ear Publishing.

Varnell, Steven (2012). "Tactical Survival", Steven Varnell Publishing.

Verification and Implementation of Language Based Deception Indicators in Civil and Criminal Narrative; Bachenko, , Joan; Fitzpatrick, Eileen; Schonwetter, Michael; Proceedings of the 22nd International Conference Linguistics, 2008.

Verónica Godoy-Cervera and Lorenzo Higueras, CRITERIA-BASED CONTENT ANALYSIS (CBCA) IN STATEMENT, Papeles del Psicólogo, 2005. Vol. 26, pp. 92-98 CREDIBILITY ASSESSMENT

Vrij, Aldert (2007). Interviewing to Detect Deception: Full Research Report.
ESRC End of Award Report, RES-000-23-0292.
Swindon: ESRC

Vrij, Aldert (2006). Statement Validity Assessment

Willis, Gordon (1994). "Cognitive Interviewing and Questionnaire Design: A
Training Manual," (Working Paper #7, National Center for Health Statistics,
Cognitive Interviewing

http://www.spyingforlying.com/2012/08/research-lyings-telltale-cluster.html

http://www.blifaloo.com/info/microexpressions.php

http://www.statementanalysis.com/cases/

http://www.lsiscan.com/reports.htm

http://content.yudu.com/Library/A17lly/BodyLanguageJULIUS FA/resources/124.htm

http://www.k-state.edu/actr/2010/12/20/suspect-interrogation-communication-strategies-and-key-personality-constructs-jessica-heuback/default.htm

http://www.footjax.com/Prop.html

http://crimeandclues.com/2013/03/02/statement-analysis-what-do-suspects-words-really-reveal/5/

http://en.wikipedia.org/wiki/False_confession

http://i-sight.com/investigation/7-ways-to-get-at-truth-in-workplace-investigation/

http://blog.al.com/birmingham-news-stories/2009/12/pelham_officers_slaying_baffle.html

http://www.tuscaloosanews.com/article/20091215/NEWS/912149930?p=1&tc=pg

http://officerphilipdavis.com/

http://en.wikipedia.org/wiki/Peripheral_vision

http://www.psychologytoday.com/experts/joe-navarro-ma

http://www.psychologytoday.com/blog/beyond-words/201110/space-invaders-the-republican-debate

http://www.nlpu.com/Articles/artic14.htm

About the Author

Steven Varnell is a law enforcement training specialist recently retired after serving over 29 years with the Florida Highway Patrol. During his career he worked Patrol, Field Training, Criminal Interdiction, SRT, and K9. He has instructed Firearms, Baton, Felony Stops, and Criminal Interdiction Courses. He was an adjunct instructor for the MCTFT Program at St. Petersburg College where he taught Highway Interdiction, Officer Safety, Patrol, and Interviews and Interrogation classes for law enforcement agencies throughout the country. He was a part of FHP's criminal interdiction pilot program which began in 1983, where he served in interdiction and K9 duties for 27 year making him one of the most experienced interdiction officers in the country.

Steve is the author of *Criminal Interdiction* and *Tactical Survival,* two widely acclaimed books available through bookstores everywhere. He is a sought out instructor and speaker in the officer safety field. Steve has started a new lecture company called Interdiction and Survival Strategies (ISS), where with former partners; together they have established a new approach to criminal based training. Steve can be reached at criminalinterdiction@live.com or go to his website at criminalinterdiction.yolasite.com. For more information and training information on the ISS group, go to: isstraining.yolasite.com.